Self-Reliance

Also by Richard Whelan

ANTHONY CARO (1974)

DOUBLE TAKE: A Comparative Look at Photographs (1981)

ROBERT CAPA: Photographs (edited with Cornell Capa) (1985)

ROBERT CAPA: A Biography (1985)

DRAWING THE LINE: The Korean War, 1950–1953 (1990)

CHILDREN OF WAR, CHILDREN OF PEACE: Photographs of Robert Capa (1991)

Self-Reliance

The Wisdom of
Ralph Waldo Emerson
as Inspiration for Daily Living

Edited and with an introduction by
Richard Whelan

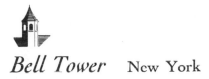

Bell Tower   New York

Published by Bell Tower, an imprint of Harmony Books, a division of Crown Publishers, Inc., 201 East 50th Street, New York, New York 10022. Member of the Crown Publishing Group.

Harmony, Bell Tower, and colophon are trademarks of Crown Publishers, Inc.

Manufactured in the United States of America

Library of Congress Cataloging-in-Publication Data
Emerson, Ralph Waldo, 1803–1882.
Self-reliance : the wisdom of Ralph Waldo Emerson as inspiration
for daily living / edited and with an introduction by Richard Whelan.
p.   cm.
I. Whelan, Richard.   II. Title.
PS1603.W43   1991
814'.3—dc20   91-11369   CIP

ISBN 0-517-58512-X
10 9 8 7 6 5

Contents

Contents

Ralph Waldo Emerson:
Biographical Note

RALPH WALDO EMERSON was born in Boston, Massachusetts, on May 25, 1803. His father, the Reverend William Emerson, who traced his descent from one of the Puritan founders of Concord, Massachusetts, was the Unitarian pastor of Boston's fashionable First Church. (As opposed to traditional Protestants, the Unitarians rejected the doctrine of the Holy Trinity; they believed that Jesus was sent by God but not that he actually *was* God. The Unitarians also rejected the Calvinist doctrine maintaining that many people are from birth destined for eternal damnation and that no efforts on their part could alter their fate.) Of the eight Emerson children, only five—all of them boys, and one of them mentally handicapped—survived infancy. Of these, RWE was the second oldest. Two of RWE's younger brothers would die in their twenties of tuberculosis.

Biographical Note

In 1811, when RWE was only eight, his father died (apparently of stomach cancer, though possibly of tuberculosis). Since he left no estate of any consequence, his wife, Ruth Haskins Emerson, was faced with the task of raising five boys in genteel poverty. Although she was assisted financially by her late husband's congregation, she was forced to open a boardinghouse to make ends meet. She was joined as head of the household by William Emerson's sister, Mary Moody Emerson, an eccentric and temperamental woman of passionately Calvinist religious convictions and practices.

From 1812 until 1817 RWE was a student at the Boston Public Latin School. In 1817, at the age of fourteen, he became the youngest member of the Harvard College class of 1821. He met his expenses by serving as the college president's orderly, by waiting on tables in the college dining room, and by teaching at his uncle Samuel Ripley's school in Waltham during college vacations. Although RWE won second prizes for essays on Socrates and on ethical philosophy, his record at Harvard was undistinguished; he graduated thirtieth in a class of fifty-nine.

RWE had long intended to follow in his father's footsteps and become a minister. However, circumstances forced him to postpone his enrollment at Harvard Divinity School for four years, during which time he taught in various secondary schools in and around Boston. Throughout that period, he was reading widely in religion and philosophy and was beginning to evolve the ideas that would be the basis for all of his later work.

RWE entered the Harvard Divinity School in 1825. Although eye troubles and rheumatism interrupted his studies, he had made sufficient progress by October 1826 to be granted an interim license to preach. The Reverend Ralph Waldo Emerson preached his first sermon that month, but almost at once he developed symptoms of tuberculosis. His uncle Samuel Ripley lent him money for a winter in Charleston, South Carolina, and St. Augustine, Florida.

Recovered, RWE returned to Boston in June 1827. He resumed his studies at Harvard and earned his living as an itinerant preacher, in which capacity he spent several weeks during December in Concord, New Hampshire. There the twenty-four-year-old RWE was captivated by a serious sixteen-year-old girl named Ellen Tucker, who was already pale from tuberculosis. Despite her illness, RWE became engaged to her the following December; they were married in September 1829. Earlier that year RWE had been ordained and was appointed junior pastor of the Second Church in Boston.

In February 1831, after only sixteen months of blissful marriage, Ellen Tucker Emerson died of tuberculosis. RWE, who had adored her and had greatly esteemed her spirituality, was devastated. The death of his "angel" led RWE to question everything, including his role as a minister, more strongly than ever. By the middle of 1832 he had decided that the sacrament of

communion was without divine authorization or effi-
cacy and that for him to continue to administer it as
such would be hypocritical. Later that year, when his
church rejected this position, he resigned from his pas-
torate and sailed for Europe. He spent much of 1833
visiting Malta, Sicily, Naples, Rome, Florence, Ven-
ice, Paris, and London. While in Britain, he managed
to meet several of his literary and philosophical heroes:
William Wordsworth, Samuel Taylor Coleridge, and
Thomas Carlyle. He was disappointed by the first two,
but he and Carlyle became lifelong friends.

Upon his return to Boston in October 1833, RWE
resumed his old occupation of itinerant preacher; during the next few years he would deliver a sermon almost every Sunday somewhere in the Boston area, or
even as far away as Plymouth or New Bedford. It was
in Plymouth that he met a devout woman named Lydia
Jackson (whom RWE always called "Lidian"). They
were married in September 1835. A modest inheritance from his late wife enabled RWE to buy a house
in Concord, Massachusetts, and provided him with a
small annual income.

In November 1833, a month after his return from
Europe, RWE delivered his first secular lecture, on
"The Uses of Natural History," to the Natural History
Society in Boston. Beginning in 1835 he would read a
new series of lectures to Boston audiences each winter.
(He never extemporized, either in the pulpit or on the
podium.) His lecture series dealt with such subjects as
the lives of great men, "English Literature," "The Phi-

losophy of History," "Human Culture," "Human Life," and "The Present Age." As his reputation spread during the 1830s, he was invited to repeat these lectures in towns near Boston.

In 1836 RWE published, anonymously, his small book entitled *Nature*, in which he articulated his philosophy of nature as the embodiment of divine law. That same year RWE's wife gave birth to a son, whom they named Waldo (the name by which RWE himself preferred to be called).

Two years later RWE delivered an address at the Harvard Divinity School, a bastion of Unitarianism, in which he attacked the spiritual and intellectual laxness of most Unitarian ministers. He would be persona non grata at Harvard for thirty years. The storm raised by the address brought about RWE's final break from the Unitarian church.

In March 1841 RWE's first series of *Essays* was published in Boston. That spring RWE invited Henry David Thoreau, a twenty-four-year-old Concord neighbor, to move into the Emerson house as handyman and gardener, in payment for which duties he would receive room and board.

January 1842 brought yet another of RWE's great tragedies: his five-year-old son, Waldo, died of scarlet fever. Two months later RWE wrote in his journal of his son's death: "I comprehend nothing of this fact but its bitterness. Explanation I have none, consolation none . . . ; only diversion; only oblivion of this, and pursuit of new objects." (At that time RWE already had two other children: Ellen, born in 1839, and Edith, born in 1841. Another child, Edward, would be born in 1844.)

In the year of his son's death, RWE had many responsibilities to distract him from his grief. He had just taken on the editorship of the Transcendentalist literary and philosophical magazine *The Dial,* and he was lecturing on an ever-widening circuit. The following year he would give lecture series in New York, Brooklyn, Philadelphia, Newark, Baltimore, Hartford, and Providence, as well as in the Boston area. Out of these lectures would come *Essays: Second Series,* published in October 1844. That year RWE bought a parcel of land on the shores of Walden Pond; the following year he would give Thoreau permission to build a cabin on that land.

Although RWE is now best known for his essays, he also wrote poetry throughout his life; in 1846 he published the first of several volumes of his poems.

In October 1847 RWE sailed for Britain, where he had been invited to give series of lectures in Liverpool, Manchester, Edinburgh, and other cities. He remained in Britain until July (except for three weeks in Paris in May), and during that time met many of the most distinguished figures in British culture and politics.

During the 1850s RWE maintained an ambitious annual schedule of lectures in cities throughout the eastern and midwestern states, speaking on such topics as "The Conduct of Life" and "English Traits," both of which series he developed into books. He also took an increasingly vocal stand in favor of the abolition of slavery. Continuing to lecture widely during the Civil War, RWE criticized Lincoln early on for seeming to be more concerned with saving the union than with abolishing slavery.

In 1866, almost thirty years after his Divinity School address that had antagonized much of the faculty, RWE was at last welcomed back to Harvard and awarded an honorary degree. He was soon elected to the university's Board of Overseers and became a leading member of the committee that was to modernize the curriculum.

The late 1860s saw RWE at the height of his career, lecturing as many as eighty times in a single year and traveling west as far as Minnesota and Iowa. By 1870, however, he was beginning to suffer serious lapses of memory. After a trip to California with his family in 1871, he made one last lecture tour of the Midwest and then retired from the platform.

In July 1872 the roof and upper stories of RWE's house were badly damaged by fire. Friends quickly raised a large sum of money to repair the house and to pay for RWE and his daughter Ellen to travel in Europe and Egypt for six months while the repairs were being undertaken. (RWE's wife chose to remain with friends in Concord.) When RWE returned to Concord in May 1873, a few days after his seventieth birthday, the entire town turned out to welcome him.

RWE died of pneumonia on April 27, 1882, and was buried in the Sleepy Hollow cemetery in Concord.

Introduction

THE YEAR 1991 marks the 150th anniversary of the original publication of Ralph Waldo Emerson's *Essays*, which contain some of the finest prose ever written in America and distill the thought of one of America's wisest thinkers. Emerson, who had left the Unitarian ministry to become an independent scholar, was himself what he said every preacher should be: "a poet smit with love of the harmonies of moral nature." He was not an academic philosopher or theologian; he was, rather, a wise man who wrote with passion and eloquence, who sought to inflame his countrymen with an understanding of life that would guarantee true freedom, dignity, and fulfillment to all.

The reader who thinks he or she is coming to Emerson for the first time will probably be surprised to discover just how familiar Emerson really is, for many of his pithiest phrases are firmly entrenched in our common parlance. Indeed, more than eight pages in Bartlett's *Familiar Quotations* are devoted to Emerson; no American is given more space.

"The disease with which the human mind now labors is the want of faith," wrote Emerson, voicing a sentiment that ever increasing numbers would echo today. He set out to rectify that situation by preaching a faith that appeals to all that is creative and generous and noble in the human spirit. In doing so, he reminds us of the essential virtues—such as love, friendship, honor, prudence, heroism, and moderation—that have, to our immeasurable loss, become all too rare in the modern world. If anything can restore these virtues to our lives, and to the conscience of our nation, it is Emerson's vision of a world "saturated with deity and with [spiritual] law."

Full of optimism and idealism, Emerson's essays make wonderful companions through the trials of life, providing a feast of inspiration and insight. Reading Emerson is like taking a potent elixir that refreshes the soul, restores hope, and inspires faith.

I have loved these essays ever since I first encountered them in college, twenty-five years ago. Through the years, whenever I felt sad or discouraged I would turn to my worn paperback, as if it were an old friend or a deeply trusted and respected mentor on whom I could count to utter the right words of solace or encouragement. Certain passages naturally became special favorites, and to facilitate finding them in my small-print edition I began to underline them. Soon I found that I had underlined so much that I could read only those passages and come away with an experience of each essay much more intense, and an understanding much clearer, than I could get if I read the entire essay. Here was the essence of Emerson, and the passages cohered as if nothing had been omitted.

I came to think of the essays as gardens in which the underlined passages were magnificent flowers — and all the rest a rampant and choking growth of nineteenth-century rhetorical weeds and vines that were best rooted out and cut back. It was then that I realized that an abridged edition of the essays could introduce Emerson, and make his down-to-earth wisdom accessible, to a readership that might otherwise be put off by his sometimes long, difficult, and overwritten passages.

To head off charges of irreverence and impertinence, let me quote an entry from Emerson's own journal, dated October 7, 1840, when he was readying his manuscript for the press:

> I have been writing with some pains essays on various matters as a sort of apology to my country for my apparent idleness. But the poor work has looked poorer daily, as I strove to end it. My genius seemed to quit me in such a mechanical work. What I write to fill up the gaps of a chapter is hard and cold, is grammar and logic; there is no magic in it; I do not wish to see it again.

Perhaps Emerson felt that he had to give his readers, accustomed to endless sermons, their money's worth. Or perhaps he felt that an important point would register only if he hammered it home through repetition and elaboration. In any case, his efforts often strain our patience and overwhelm the beauty, the clarity, and the power of the original insight. But when the "hard and cold" passages are stripped away, the magic of what remains is revealed all the more clearly.

To cite an extreme case, the essay entitled "Manners" could easily—without loss, and indeed with gain—be reduced to a single one of its sentences: "Defect in manners is usually the defect of fine perceptions." That is to say, we would treat our fellow human beings better if we more clearly recognized that the divine spirit operates through them. It is the spirit, not rank or wealth, that deserves our respect. As Emerson put it in a February 1836 journal entry, "God manifest in the flesh of every man is a perfect rule of social life. Justify yourself to an infinite Being in the ostler and dandy and stranger, and you shall never repent." And yet Emerson fails to articulate any such explanation in his essay. Instead, he launches into an elaborate (and stultifying) disquisition on gentlemen, courtesy, and fashion. It is a tour de force, but that is precisely my point. The essay is forced; it is "hard and cold," and "there is no magic in it." That essay, along with several others, has been omitted from this edition.

What remains is the essence of Emerson. Open this edition to any page and you will discover the glories of Emerson's wisdom and eloquence. Much of his meaning is self-evident, and his greatest passages stand very firmly on their own. But for those readers who would like to gain some understanding of Emerson's philosophy as a whole, the following pages may provide a framework within which to read the essays.

EMERSON'S PHILOSOPHY

Emerson believed that a power, which can only be called divine, permeates every atom of the universe and that the unchanging nature of that power determines every detail of human life, of history, and of the natural world. That is so because the universe and everything in it form a single, unified, organic system that is the self-expression of the Universal Soul, God, the ONE. (Emerson used the term "God" to mean not a personlike deity but rather an abstract power.) The material universe was created by, and is totally pervaded by, the Universal Soul and is, in effect, the body in which it resides and through which it acts.

Furthermore, the structure of every particle implies the structure of the whole. The basic laws, the universal truths, are inherent in every substance, being, and event. If you view any part with sufficient understanding, you will grasp the nature of the whole. Emerson passionately believed that if you understand that basic fact "every moment instructs, and every object: for wisdom is infused into every form." ("Nature") Indeed, developing that claim to its fullest force, Emerson boldly asserted that "the world exists for the education of each man."

"Every chemical substance, every plant, every animal in its growth," marveled Emerson, "teaches the unity of cause, the variety of appearance." ("History") What he advocated was a life that would be lived in full and constant awareness of that "unity of cause." The wise person, then, is one who looks *through* the phenomena of the material world and sees behind them the divine spirit, the supreme intelligence and its laws—the Idea that shapes and guides. It is in that sense that Emerson called himself an Idealist. And because he believed that the Idea transcends its material manifestations, he also referred to himself as a Transcendentalist.

Emerson felt that the main tenets of his philosophy were so self-evident that no one of true intelligence and sensitivity could fail to arrive at them. "We learn that God IS," he exulted; "that he is in me; and that all things are shadows of him." At those moments when the individual soul, which is God, dominates your consciousness and determines your actions, then you not only perform an act of deepest reverence but actually participate in the divine. As Emerson wrote, "The simplest person who in his integrity worships God becomes God." ("Over-Soul") In other words, "God in us worships God." (*Journal,* July 15, 1831)

The Universal Soul is the ultimate Self— absolutely independent, totally spontaneous, supremely intelligent and powerful. It is utterly Self-Reliant. Reflecting the Universal Soul's essence, the universe is an infinitely self-adjusting, self-regulating system. It is always in a state of dynamic equilibrium. As Emerson observed, "A perfect equity adjusts its balance in all parts of life. The dice of God are always loaded. The world looks like a multiplication table or a mathematical equation, which, turn it how you will, balances itself." ("Compensation")

Emerson was an optimist, and he firmly believed that the divine spirit is benevolent. "All nature," he declared, "is the rapid efflux of goodness executing and organizing itself." ("Circles") Evil is only a surface phenomenon; the wise person, who sees the profound truth, understands that good is always ultimately triumphant. Nowhere is that optimism more clearly expressed than in a passage from Emerson's essay on the sixteenth-century French philosopher Michel de Montaigne (included in Emerson's book *Representative Men*), which speaks directly to the discouragement that is so difficult to avoid today as we look around us at a world in which corruption and violence often seem to have the upper hand.

> Things seem to tend downward, to justify despondency, to promote rogues, to defeat the just; and *[yet]* by knaves, as by martyrs, the just cause is carried forward. Although knaves win in every political struggle, although society seems to be delivered over

from the hands of one set of criminals into the hands of another set of criminals as fast as the government is changed, and the march of civilization is a train of felonies, yet the general ends are somehow answered. We see, now, events forced on, which seem to retard or retrograde the civility of ages. But the world-spirit is a good swimmer, and storms and waves cannot drown him. He snaps his fingers at laws: and so, throughout history, heaven seems to affect low and poor means. Through toys and atoms, a great and beneficent tendency irresistibly streams.

Elsewhere Emerson put that idea more concisely and enigmatically when he said, "Let the victory fall where it will, we are on that side." ("Nature") He meant that what happens is always for the best of the Universal Soul, and whatever benefits it benefits all of its embodiments. Having faith in that immutable fact, our soul "calms itself with knowing that all things go well." ("Self-Reliance")

Each of us is potentially a microcosm of the relationship between the Universal Soul and the universe; the central challenge in life is to realize that potential as fully as possible. The key is the knowledge that you are pervaded by the Universal Self, that God is in everyone and everything. When you see God in all the workings of the world, then you will naturally have faith that all that happens is for the best. For example, as bitter as they may be, crisis and tragedy are often the most powerful catalysts for positive change.

The more fully you recognize those truths, and the more constantly you can act with them in mind, the more you become like the Universal Soul, which is to say that you become more self-reliant. When you are self-reliant, you fulfill the divine potential within yourself. You emulate God, and there can be no higher good than that.

FAITH IN THE UNIVERSAL SOUL is the key to fulfillment. If you have such faith, your life becomes filled with spiritual light. You then act with the wisdom, courage, strength, and love that such light bestows.

When you recognize the Universal Soul in all persons and all events, you are enlightened, which is to say that you live in the light. It is that simple. You needn't study Sanskrit or pursue an esoteric regimen of meditation and self-denial in order to become enlightened. Indeed, such exercises are all too often ways of postponing enlightenment, which is always in the here and now of the ordinary and the everyday. It is natural to be enlightened—and unnatural not to be.

If you live in the light, you will go through life with a feeling of security, for you will have a sense of prosperity and well-being that does not depend upon your material circumstances. But those who refuse to acknowledge the divine presence condemn themselves to a barren life, regardless of their accomplishments. "If he have not found his home in God, his manners, his forms of speech, the turn of his sentences, the build, shall I say, of all his opinions, will involuntarily confess it, let him brave it out how he will. If he have found his center, the Deity will shine through him, through all the disguises of ignorance, of ungenial temperament, of unfavorable circumstance." ("Over-Soul")

The person who acknowledges the divine spirit "will weave no longer a spotted life of shreds and patches, but he will live with a divine unity. He will cease from what is base and frivolous in his life, and be content with all places and any service he can render. He will calmly front the morrow in the negligency of that trust which carries God with it, and so hath already the whole future in the bottom of the heart." ("Over-Soul")

ONE OF EMERSON'S CENTRAL CONCEPTS is that each of us must obey the divine voice within himself or herself. But how do we recognize the voice of God within us? How do we recognize truth when it is revealed to us by the soul? "The soul is the perceiver and revealer of truth. We know truth when we see it, let skeptic and scoffer say what they choose. Foolish people ask you, when you have spoken what they do not wish to hear, 'How do you know it is the truth, and not an error of your own?' We know truth when we

see it, from opinion, as we know when we are awake."
("Over-Soul")

We recognize truth when it comes to us because
the Universal Soul has endowed us with the faculties
necessary for such recognition. When we perceive a
truth—whether it is a universal principle or merely the
solution to a personal dilemma—it is like an insight
erupting into consciousness with such force and per-
suasiveness that it seems as though we heard it from
another. What Emerson describes may in fact be a
matter of each person's gaining access to his or her
unconscious. He would say that "the unconscious" is
simply another name for the Universal Soul within us.

God is within us, and revelation is the Universal
Soul speaking to us and through us. To use an embar-
rassingly simplistic and anachronistic, but I hope helpful, analogy, we might say that the divine spirit is like
a radio station. We spend much of our time acting as
if we were poorly tuned radios, our reception of the
divine signal more or less obscured by the interference
of static or of other stations. When we finally adjust
our tuning properly, the signal is loud and clear, and
its message inspiring and motivating.

The best way to tune in clearly to the divine signal
is to listen in quiet reflection. It was in order to find
such quiet that Emerson advocated periods of solitude.
He prescribed no method or formula, but he recom-
mended silent contemplation or meditation, thoughtful
study, and communing with nature. He found that
revelation came readily in quiet but was more difficult

to find, and to put into practice, amid the noise and the jostling of our daily business. "The voices which we hear in solitude grow faint and inaudible as we enter into the world." ("Self-Reliance")

During the 1830s Emerson was greatly influenced by the Quakers, at whose meetings for worship everyone sits in silence waiting for the Inner Voice, the Inner Light. When you are literally inspired, you rise to speak, which is to say that you allow the divine spirit to voice its wisdom through you. The insights that are found in the silence are referred to as "messages" from the divine spirit. They can be very simple or very profound, very abstract or very anecdotal.

We do not deserve credit for the truths that are articulated through us any more than a radio can be given credit for a program that it receives. "We lie in the lap of immense intelligence, which makes us organs of its activity and receivers of its truth. When we discern justice, when we discern truth, we do nothing of ourselves but allow a passage to its beams." ("Self-Reliance")

The greater a work of art or a scientific discovery, the more fully the artist or scientist has allowed the Universal Soul to speak through him or her. In one of his poems, in lines that are inscribed on his tombstone, Emerson summed up the receptive nature of the highest creativity:

> The passive master lent his hand
> To the vast soul that o'er him planned.

EMERSON MAINTAINED that speaking the truth, as you see it, is an act of reverence, as is respecting the infinite interpretations and applications of truth by others. He deplored the tendency of people "to pair off into insane parties, and learn the amount of truth each knows by the denial of an equal amount of truth." ("The Conservative")

If you live in the light, you will keep an open mind, and your faith will not be threatened by new discoveries and insights. "Valor consists in self-recovery. . . . This can only be by his preferring truth to his past apprehension of truth, and his alert acceptance of it from whatever quarter." ("Circles") In the service of truth, you must be willing to endure the scorn of those "little minds" that cherish "a foolish consistency." ("Self-Reliance") "If you would be a man, speak today what you think today in words as hard as cannon-balls, and tomorrow speak what tomorrow thinks in hard words again, though it contradict everything you said today." ("Self-Reliance")

One of Emerson's guiding principles was: avoid the company of persons with whom you cannot be totally forthright. Be sincere or be silent. Speak the whole truth, as you see it, or do not speak at all. Emerson maintained that it is better to be alone than to be surrounded by people with whom you cannot be truly and fully yourself.

Emerson valued sincerity above all other virtues.

Introduction

To be sincere is to express, honestly and directly, the essence of your personality in response to the circumstances of the present moment. To be sincere is to reject the secondhand, the merely conventional, and the arbitrary, and to despise hypocrisy, cant, and prejudice. It is to be true to yourself, both in thought and in expression. It is to Be, and not merely to Seem. To be sincere is to fulfill your God-given potential and to accept your God-given role.

To be sincere, in Emerson's view, is thus to perform an act of reverence to the divine spirit. That is the central paradox of Emerson's individualism: to be sincere (which is to say, to be a true individual) is to eschew selfishness and self-indulgence; to be sincere is to allow the divine spirit to express itself through the individual. As Emerson stated, "Self-reliance, the height and perfection of man, is reliance on God."

Emerson exhorts each of us to embrace fully the unique and concrete reality of his or her existence—the intersection of specific talents and limitations with specific circumstances. And he counsels us not to waste our lives in wishing that we were other than what we are.

> There is a time in every man's education when he arrives at the conviction that envy is ignorance; that imitation is suicide; that he must take himself for better, for worse, as his portion. . . . Trust thyself: every heart vibrates to that iron string. Accept the place the divine Providence has found for you: the so-

ciety of your contemporaries, the connection
of events. ("Self-Reliance")

In light of our real possibilities, each of us must do
what he or she can do most effectively and fulfillingly.
Our actual circumstances dictate which aspects of our
potential will be utilized and developed. As the Span-
ish philosopher José Ortega y Gasset put it, "I am
myself and my circumstances."

Emerson taught that the divine spirit manifests
itself through our evolving circumstances. Therefore,
the enlightened life is a constant process of responding
intelligently to the immediate specifics of reality. The
practical thrust of Emerson's individualism is: if you
cannot do what you want, then you must learn to want
what you can do.

Each of us should always attempt to focus on the
good that the present moment has to offer. "Without
any shadow of doubt, amidst this vertigo of shows and
politics, I settle myself ever the firmer in the creed that
we should not postpone and refer and wish, but do
broad justice where we are, by whomsoever we deal
with, accepting our actual companions and circumstances, however humble or odious, as the mystic officials to whom the universe has delegated its whole
pleasure for us." ("Experience")

"Do not waste yourself in rejection," wrote Emerson; "do not bark against the bad, but chant the
beauty of the good." (*Journal,* July 1841) Dwell on
your dissatisfaction and you will come away empty-

handed when you might have received considerable benefit or pleasure, though perhaps not of the sort, or in the degree, that you had hoped for. If you always concentrate on what you don't have and are constantly preoccupied with getting more, you will end up with nothing of real value.

By no means is Emerson advising either servile passivity or dispirited resignation. Nor does he mean that you should not try to improve your circumstances if they are oppressive or unsatisfying—as long as that effort does not blind you to the positive aspects of the present. Life is to be lived in the here and now. To do otherwise is, quite simply, to live less than fully. Furthermore, whatever our circumstances, it is our responsibility to recognize the divine spirit in all persons and in all events. To see your neighbor as a manifestation of the divine spirit is to love your neighbor.

When you live in the light, you understand that life's greatest pleasure is to be able to see the extraordinariness of what may appear to others as merely ordinary, to see all of history and human nature in the everyday, and the divine spirit in the mundane. We should, therefore, as Emerson put it with great poetry, attempt to dwell "in the earnest experience of the common day—by reason of the present moment and the mere trifle having become porous to thought, and bibulous of the sea of light." ("Over-Soul")

Emerson was not, however, insensitive to the terrible sense of frustration that can so easily poison a life. In his essay about Montaigne he wrote:

The divine Providence . . . has shown the heaven and earth to every child and filled him with a desire for the whole; a desire raging, infinite; a hunger, as of space to be filled with planets; a cry of famine, as of devils for souls. Then, for the satisfaction, to each man is administered a single drop, a bead of dew of vital power, *per day*—a cup as large as space, and one drop of the water of life in it.

One of the greatest challenges facing every human being is the need to overcome the rage that such torture entails. By learning to accept—with resignation if not with total equanimity—the vast discrepancy between our desires and reality, we perform the ultimate act of faith in the unfathomable wisdom of the divine spirit.

WHEN TALENT AND OPPORTUNITY MESH, then you know that you have found your vocation. The discovery of the talent of which this is true is far more a matter of acquiescence than of ambition.

A little consideration of what takes place around us every day would show us that a higher law than that of our will regulates events . . . that only in our easy, simple, spontaneous action are we strong, and by

contenting ourselves with obedience we become divine. ("Spiritual Laws")

Such obedience is simultaneously self-abnegation
and self-fulfillment.

Of course, the actual carrying out of the divine
imperatives demands effort, self-discipline, persever-
ance, and courage. But if you live in the light, the
divine spirit will supply you with those qualities along
with its imperatives, for *true* understanding carries
such force that it does not remain intellectual; we feel
compelled to put our insight into action at once. "The
power to see is not separated from the will to do."
("Over-Soul")

Once we have understood that the divine spirit
acts through us, if we allow it to do so, then we feel a
great responsibility always to be open to its promptings and to put them into action. But we are also given
a great sense of security in knowing that we are simply
agents of God. In the awareness that God is acting
through us, we find determination, courage, and
strength. What we might be too timid, or too lazy, to
do for ourselves, we do for God within us.

A PERSON WHO LOVES THE DIVINE SPIRIT
is wise and virtuous, loving, sincere, honorable, self-
reliant, self-disciplined, generous, and nonviolent.
Such a person acts responsibly and reasonably, and

does what needs to be done. He or she is capable of governing himself or herself, not only morally but also politically.

That conclusion was taken for granted by the Founding Fathers of the United States, and it underlay all of Emerson's philosophy. Only *self*-governing (i.e., self-reliant, self-disciplined) people are able to be self-*governing* in the political sense. A democracy ignores that absolutely basic and eternal truth at peril to its very existence. Now, when so much of American culture is based on greed, self-indulgence, ignorance, and viciously destructive passion, we must understand that a nation in which a majority of the people is enslaved and degraded by such a culture will automatically lose its ability to govern itself democratically.

Yielding to selfish impulses and appetites condemns one to bondage and oppression, for when blind selfishness becomes dominant, chaos results; in reaction to chaos, nations have always resorted to highly authoritarian—indeed, absolutist—governments in the hope that they would impose and maintain law and order. The self-discipline, self-control, reasonableness, and moderation that have their roots in the love of the divine spirit provide the keys to freedom—the *only* keys to *true* freedom. That is an essential aspect of Emerson's message. Now, more than ever, we need to listen to him.

Introduction

THE ESSENCE OF EMERSON'S PHILOSOPHY could be summed up thus: every person is capable of direct access to the Universal Soul and thus to universal truth. Far and away the most important task in life—indeed, perhaps the whole point of life—is for each of us to strive to develop that access so that the insights it provides will govern all our thoughts and actions. In a nutshell: love the Universal Soul and be spontaneous.

Spiritual growth and personal development are inherent in every life that is lived in awareness of the divine spirit working through us. The great adventure of life is to discover how the spirit will express itself through us and along what paths it will lead us. As Emerson says of every person: "The power which resides in him is new in nature, and none but he knows what that is which he can do, nor does he know until he has tried." ("Self-Reliance")

"The highest revelation," wrote Emerson in his journal, "is that God is in every man." He believed that every individual soul is an inlet of the Universal Soul, and every person is a vessel of the divine light, even if he or she doesn't allow that light to shine forth. When we heed the promptings of our soul—which is to say, when we act in such a way as to honor the divine spirit in ourselves and in every other person—then we allow the spirit to act through us.

Emerson's *Essays* constitute a set of variations on these basic themes. Each essay develops the author's fundamental concepts in relation to a different aspect of life, but those subjects are so deeply related that all of the essays convey essentially the same message. Emerson had no interest in fabricating an elaborate philosophical theory. Instead, he was content to examine a few vital truths — those that apply to life as we actually live it. He looked at those truths as if he were handling beautiful objects, turning each one to study it from every angle, savoring all of its qualities, and communicating the pleasures he derived from his observations. No philosopher has ever written more eloquently or more compellingly about how to live a life filled with spiritual light.

A Note on the Text

THE TEXT OF THE ESSAYS printed here from Emerson's *Essays: First Series* (originally published in 1841 simply as *Essays*) is based primarily on the second edition of that work (1847), for which Emerson had carefully revised and corrected the first edition. In revising his text, Emerson deleted many redundant phrases and sentences and, in other cases, clarified some phrasings. Sometimes, however, he went too far, transforming the poetry of the first edition into prose in the second. For the present edition, the editor has returned, wherever necessary, to the original version. In the case of *Essays: Second Series*, however, its first edition (1844) is the most satisfactory.

The contents and sequence of the two series of *Essays* as originally published are as follows:

A Note on the Text

I have omitted in their entirety the essays entitled "Love," "Art," "The Poet," and "Nominalist and Realist," as well as "Manners" and the lecture "New England Reformers." In each case I felt that neither the content nor the style measured up to the standard set by the other essays.

I have also added a lecture, "The Transcendentalist," which is not usually included in editions of Emerson's *Essays*. Emerson originally published "The Transcendentalist" in his book *Nature; Addresses, and Lectures* (1849).

I have not held to the order in which the essays appeared in their original editions. I have rearranged them so that the reader begins with the essays that state Emerson's major ideas most clearly and forcefully. Within some essays I have also rearranged the sequence of some blocks of text to create a more logical flow of ideas.

In the interest of readability, I have made some minor textual changes that do not in any way distort the spirit of the text. By far the greatest number of these changes involve punctuation, which I have modernized when I felt that Emerson's usage might confuse the reader or call undue attention to itself. In some other cases (again, only where unnecessary confusion might otherwise result) I have substituted the modern equivalent of a word used by Emerson; the most notable instance of this is in those cases in which Emerson used the word *somewhat* where we would today say *something* (as in: "There is somewhat wonderful about . . ."). I have used the modern spelling of proper names: *Shakespeare*, for example, instead of Emerson's habitual *Shakspeare*. Emerson was inconsistent in his spelling of such words as *neighborhood*, which he also spelled *neighbourhood*. I have opted for the modern American spellings throughout.

Wherever I have supplied an occasional word to aid comprehension, those additions are placed in brackets and set in italics. Since Emerson could be as inventive and idiosyncratic in his usage as Emily Dickinson, I have inserted a brief explanation immediately following some particularly cryptic phrases and sentences. Such explanations are also placed in brackets and set in italics.

I have not employed ellipses to indicate where I have omitted text or have joined together parts of sentences. When I have deleted the opening words or phrases of a sentence, I have supplied an uppercase initial letter without brackets. In general, a space break with an ornament indicates the omission of a sizable block of text, but in some cases I have supplied such a break where Emerson suddenly shifts the course of his thoughts. Such a shift may come in the middle of a paragraph of the original text. In other instances, where Emerson's shifts are less drastic, I have simply broken one of his run-on paragraphs into two or more paragraphs.

Let me assure the reader that although all of the above may make it sound as though I have changed Emerson beyond recognition, that is by no means the case. All of my changes have been to make Emerson more accessible to the modern reader and to allow not only his wisdom but also his voice to come through as clearly as possible.

THE ESSAYS

Spiritual Laws

A LITTLE CONSIDERATION of what takes place around us every day would show us that a higher law than that of our will regulates events; that our painful labors are very unnecessary and altogether fruitless; that only in our easy, simple, spontaneous action are we strong, and by contenting ourselves with obedience we become divine. Belief and love — a believing love will relieve us of a vast load of care. O my brothers, God exists. There is a soul at the center of nature, and over the will of every man, so that none of us can wrong the universe. It has so infused its strong enchantment into nature that we prosper when we accept its advice; and when we struggle to wound its creatures, our hands are glued to our sides, or they beat our own breasts.

The whole course of things goes to teach us faith. We need only obey. There is guidance for each of us, and by lowly listening we shall hear the right word. Why need you choose so painfully your place, and occupation, and associates, and modes of action and of entertainment? Certainly there is a possible right for us that precludes the need of balance and willful election. For you there is a reality, a fit place and congenial duties. Place yourself in the middle of the stream of power and wisdom which flows into you as life, place yourself in the full center of that flood, then you are without effort impelled to truth, to right, and a perfect contentment.

I say, *do not choose;* but that is a figure of speech by which I would distinguish what is commonly called *choice* among men, and which is a partial act, the choice of the hands, of the eye, of the appetites, and not a whole act of the man. But that which I call right or goodness is the choice of my constitution; and that which I call heaven, and inwardly aspire after, is the state of circumstance desirable to my constitution; and the action which I in all my years tend to do is the work for my faculties. We must hold a man amenable to reason for the choice of his daily craft or profession. It is not an excuse any longer for his deeds that they are the custom of his trade. What business has he with an evil trade? Has he not a *calling* in his character?

Each man has his own vocation. The talent is the call. There is one direction in which all space is open to him. He has faculties silently inviting him thither to endless exertion. He is like a ship in a river; he runs against obstructions on every side but one; on that side all obstruction is taken away, and he sweeps serenely over a deepening channel into an infinite sea. This talent and this call depend on his organization, or the mode in which the general soul incarnates itself in him. He inclines to do something which is easy to him, and good when it is done, but which no other man can do. He has no rival. For the more truly he consults his own powers, the more difference will his work exhibit from the work of any other.

His ambition is exactly proportioned to his powers. The height of the pinnacle is determined by the breadth of the base. Every man has this call of the power to do something unique, and no man has any other call. The pretence that he has another call, a summons by name and personal election and outward "signs that mark him extraordinary and not in the roll of common men" is fanaticism, and betrays obtuseness to perceive that there is one mind in all the individuals, and no respect of persons therein.

By doing his work, he makes the need felt which he can supply, and creates the taste by which he is enjoyed. By doing his own work, he unfolds himself.

OUR MORAL NATURE is vitiated by any interference of our will. People represent virtue as a struggle, and take to themselves great airs upon their attainments; and the question is everywhere vexed, when a noble nature is commended, whether the man is not better who strives with temptation? But there is no merit in the matter. Either God is there, or he is not there. We love characters in proportion as they are impulsive and spontaneous. The less a man thinks or knows about his virtues, the better we like him.

Not less conspicuous is the preponderance of nature over will in all practical life. There is less intention in history than we ascribe to it. We impute deep-laid, far-sighted plans to Caesar and Napoleon; but the best of their power was in nature, not in them. Men of an extraordinary success, in their honest moments, have always sung, "Not unto us, not unto us." According to the faith of their times, they have built altars to Fortune or to Destiny, or to St. Julian. Their success lay in their parallelism to the course of thought, which found in them an unobstructed channel; and the wonders of which they were the visible conductors seemed to the eye their deed. Did the wires generate the galvanism? It is even true that there was less in them on which they could reflect than in another; as the virtue of a pipe is to be smooth and hollow. That which externally seemed will and immovableness, was willingness and self-annihilation.

The great man knew not that he was great. It took a century or two for that fact to appear. What he did, he did because he must; it was the most natural thing in the world, and grew out of the circumstances of the moment.

THE SOUL WILL NOT KNOW either deformity or pain. If, in the hours of clear reason, we should speak the severest truth, we should say that we had never made a sacrifice. In these hours the mind seems so great that nothing can be taken from us that seems much. All loss, all pain, is particular; the universe remains to the heart unhurt. Neither vexations nor calamities abate our trust. No man ever stated his griefs as lightly as he might. Allow for exaggeration in the most patient and sorely ridden hack that ever was driven. For it is only the finite that has wrought and suffered; the infinite lies stretched in smiling repose.

THE INTELLECTUAL LIFE may be kept clean and healthful if man will live the life of nature and not import into his mind difficulties which are none of his. No man need be perplexed in his speculations. Let him do and say what strictly belongs to him, and, though very ignorant of books, his nature shall not yield him any intellectual obstructions and doubts.

THE LESSON IS FORCIBLY TAUGHT by these observations that our life might be easier and simpler than we make it; that the world might be a happier place than it is; that there is no need of struggles, convulsions, and despairs, of the wringing of the hands and the gnashing of the teeth; that we miscreate our own evils. We interfere with the optimism of nature; for, whenever we get this vantage-ground of the past, or of a wiser mind in the present, we are able to discern that we are begirt with spiritual laws which execute themselves.

The face of external nature teaches the same lesson with calm superiority. Nature will not have us fret and fume. She does not like our benevolence or our learning much better than she likes our frauds and wars. When we come out of the caucus, or the bank, or the Abolition-convention, or the Temperance-meeting, or the Transcendental club, into the fields and woods, she says to us, "So hot? my little sir."

IF WE LOOK WIDER, things are all alike; laws, and letters, and creeds, and modes of living, seem a travesty of truth. Our society is encumbered by ponderous machinery, which resembles the endless aqueducts which the Romans built over hill and dale, and which are superseded by the discovery of the law that water rises to the level of its source. It is a Chinese wall, which any nimble Tartar can leap over. It is a standing army, not so good as a peace. It is a graduated, titled, richly appointed Empire, quite superfluous when town-meetings are found to answer just as well.

Let us draw a lesson from nature, which always works by short ways. When the fruit is ripe, it falls. When the fruit is dispatched, the leaf falls.

The simplicity of the universe is very different from the simplicity of a machine. He who sees moral nature out and out, and thoroughly knows how knowledge is acquired and character formed, is a pedant. The simplicity of nature is not that which may easily be read, but is inexhaustible. The last analysis can no wise be made. We judge of a man's wisdom by his hope, knowing that the perception of the inexhaustibleness of nature is an immortal youth.

WHAT A MAN DOES, that he has. What has he to do with hope or fear? In himself is his might. Let him regard no good as solid but that which is in his nature, and which must grow out of him as long as he exists. The goods of fortune may come and go like summer leaves; let him scatter them on every wind as the momentary signs of his infinite productiveness.

Spiritual Laws

A MAN'S GENIUS, the quality that differences him
from every other, the susceptibility to one class of influences, the selection of what is fit for him, the rejection of what is unfit, determines for him the character
of the universe. A man is a method, a progressive
arrangement; a selecting principle, gathering his like
to him, wherever he goes. He takes only his own, out
of the multiplicity that sweeps and circles round him.
He is like one of those booms which are set out from
the shore on rivers to catch driftwood, or like the lode-
stone amongst splinters of steel.

Those facts, words, persons, which dwell in his
memory without his being able to say why, remain,
because they have a relation to him not less real for
being as yet unapprehended. They are symbols of value
to him, as they can interpret parts of his consciousness
which he would vainly seek words for in the conventional images of books and other minds. What attracts
my attention shall have it, as I will go to the man who
knocks at my door, while a thousand persons as worthy go by it, to whom I give no regard. It is enough
that these particulars speak to me. A few anecdotes, a
few traits of character, manners, face, a few incidents,
have an emphasis in your memory out of all proportion
to their apparent significance, if you measure them by
the ordinary standards. They relate to your gift. Let
them have their weight, and do not reject them, and
cast about for illustration and facts more usual in literature. Respect them, for they have their origin in
deepest nature. What your heart thinks great is great.
The soul's emphasis is always right.

A MUTUAL UNDERSTANDING is ever the firm-
est chain. Nothing seems so easy as to speak and to be
understood. Yet a man may come to find *that* the strongest of defences and of ties—that he has been understood; and he who has received an opinion may come
to find it the most inconvenient of bonds.

If a teacher have any opinion which he wishes to
conceal, his pupils will become as fully indoctrinated
into that as into any which he publishes. If you pour
water into a vessel twisted into coils and angles, it is
vain to say, I will pour it only into this or that; it will
find its level in all. Men feel and act the conse-
quences of your doctrine without being able to show
how they follow. Show us an arc of the curve, and a
good mathematician will find out the whole figure.
We are always reasoning from the seen to the un-
seen. Hence the perfect intelligence that subsists between wise men of remote ages. A man cannot bury
his meanings so deep in his book, but time and like-
minded men will find them.

No man can learn what he has not preparation for
learning, however near to his eyes is the object. A
chemist may tell his most precious secrets to a carpen-
ter, and he shall be never the wiser—the secrets he
would not utter to a chemist for an estate. God screens
us evermore from premature ideas. Our eyes are
holden that we cannot see things that stare us in the
face, until the hour arrives when the mind is ripened;

then we behold them, and the time when we saw them not is like a dream.

Not in nature but in man is all the beauty and worth he sees. The world is very empty, and is indebted to this gilding, exalting soul for all its pride. "My children," said an old man to his boys scared by a figure in the dark entry, "my children, you will never see anything worse than yourselves." As in dreams, so in the scarcely less fluid events of the world, every man sees himself in colossal, without knowing that it is himself. The good which he sees, compared to the evil which he sees, is as his own good to his own evil. What can we see or acquire but what we are? You have observed a skilful man reading Virgil. Well, that author is a thousand books to a thousand persons. Take the book into your two hands, and read your eyes out; you will never find what I find.

WE FOOLISHLY THINK, in our days of sin, that we must court friends by compliance to the customs of society, to its dress, its breeding, and its estimates. But only that soul can be my friend which I encounter on the line of my own march, that soul to which I do not decline, and which does not decline to me, but, native of the same celestial latitude, repeats in its own all my experience.

The same reality pervades all teaching. The man may teach by doing, and not otherwise. If he can communicate himself, he can teach, but not by words. He teaches who gives, and he learns who receives. There is no teaching until the pupil is brought into the same state or principle in which you are; a transfusion takes place: he is you, and you are he; then is a teaching, and by no unfriendly chance or bad company can he ever quite lose the benefit. But your propositions run out of one ear as they ran in at the other.

THE EFFECT OF ANY WRITING on the public mind is mathematically measurable by its depth of thought. How much water does it draw? If it awaken you to think, if it lift you from your feet with the great voice of eloquence, then the effect is to be wide, slow, permanent, over the minds of men. If the pages instruct you not, they will die like flies in the hour. The way to speak and write that shall not go out of fashion is to speak and write sincerely. That statement only is fit to be made public which you have come at in attempting to satisfy your own curiosity.

Life alone can impart life; and though we should burst, we can only be valued as we make ourselves valuable. There is no luck in literary reputation. They who make up the final verdict upon every book are not the partial and noisy readers of the hour when it appears; but a court as of angels, a public not to be bribed, not to be entreated, and not to be overawed, decides upon every man's title to fame. Only those books come down which deserve to last. Gilt edges, vellum, and morocco, and presentation-copies to all the libraries, will not preserve a book in circulation beyond its intrinsic date.

HUMAN CHARACTER evermore publishes itself. The most fugitive deed and word, the mere air of doing a thing, the intimated purpose, expresses character. If you act, you show character; if you sit still, if you sleep, you show it. You think, because you have spoken nothing when others spoke, and have given no opinion on the times, on the church, on slavery, on marriage, on socialism, on secret societies, on the college, on parties and persons, that your verdict is still expected with curiosity as a reserved wisdom. Far otherwise; your silence answers very loud. You have no oracle to utter, and your fellow men have learned that you cannot help them; for oracles speak. Doth not wisdom cry, and understanding put forth her voice?

A man passes for what he is worth. Very idle is all curiosity concerning other people's estimate of us, and all fear of remaining unknown is not less so. If a man

know that he can do any thing—that he can do it
better than anyone else—he has a pledge of the ac-
knowledgment of that fact by all persons.

As much virtue as there is, so much appears; as
much goodness as there is, so much reverence it commands. All the devils respect virtue. The high, the
generous, the self-devoted sect will always instruct and
command mankind. Never was a sincere word utterly
lost. Never a magnanimity fell to the ground but there
is some heart to greet and accept it unexpectedly. A
man passes for what he is worth. What he is engraves
itself on his face, on his form, on his fortunes, in letters
of light. Concealment avails him nothing; boasting,
nothing. There is confession in the glances of our eyes,
in our smiles, in salutations, and the grasp of hands.
His sin bedaubs him, mars all his good impression.
Men know not why they do not trust him. His vice
glasses his eye, cuts lines of mean expression in his
cheek, pinches the nose, sets the mark of the beast on
the back of the head, and writes, O fool! fool! on the
forehead of a king.

If you would not be known to do any thing, never
do it. On the other hand, the hero fears not that, if he
withhold the avowal of a just and brave act, it will go
unwitnessed and unloved. One knows it—himself—
and is pledged by it to sweetness of peace, and to
nobleness of aim, which will prove in the end a better
proclamation of it than the relating of the incident.

Virtue is the adherence in action to the nature of
things, and the nature of things makes it prevalent. It

consists in a perpetual substitution of being for seeming, and with sublime propriety God is described as saying, I AM.

The lesson which all these observations convey is, Be, and not seem.

THE OBJECT OF THE MAN is to make daylight shine through him, to suffer the law to traverse his whole being without obstruction, so that, on whatever point soever of his doing your eye falls, it shall report truly of his character, whether it be his diet, his house, his religious forms, his society, his mirth, his vote, his opposition.

WHY SHOULD WE MAKE IT A POINT with our false modesty to disparage that man we are, and that form of being assigned to us? A good man is contented.

I desire not to disgrace the soul. The fact that I am here certainly shows me that the soul had need of an organ here. Shall I not assume the post? Shall I skulk and dodge and duck with my unseasonable apologies and vain modesty, and imagine my being here impertinent?

LET A MAN BELIEVE IN GOD, and not in names and places and persons. Let the great soul incarnated in some woman's form, poor and sad and single, in some Dolly or Joan, go out to service, and sweep chambers and scour floors, and its effulgent daybeams cannot be muffled or hid, but to sweep and scour will instantly appear supreme and beautiful actions, the top and radiance of human life, and all people will get mops and brooms; until, lo! suddenly the great soul has enshrined itself in some other form, and done some other deed, and that is now the flower and head of all living nature. We know the authentic effects of the true fire through every one of its million disguises.

The Over-Soul

MAN IS A STREAM whose source is hidden. Always our being is descending into us from we know not whence. The most exact calculator has no prescience that something incalculable may not balk the very next moment. I am constrained every moment to acknowledge a higher origin for events than the will I call mine.

As with events, so it is with thoughts. When I watch that flowing river, which, out of regions I see not, pours for a season its streams into me, I see that I am a pensioner—not a cause, but a surprised spectator of this ethereal water—that I desire and look up, and put myself in the attitude of reception, but from some alien energy the visions come.

The Supreme Critic on all errors of the past and the present, and the only prophet of that which must be, is that great nature in which we rest, as the earth lies in the soft arms of the atmosphere; that Unity, that Over-Soul, within which every man's particular being is contained and made one with all other; that common heart, of which all sincere conversation is the worship, to which all right action is submission; that overpowering reality which confutes our tricks and talents, and constrains every one to pass for what he is, and to speak from his character and not from his tongue; and which evermore tends to pass into our thought and hand, and become wisdom, and virtue, and power, and beauty.

We live in succession, in division, in parts, in particles. Meantime, within man is the soul of the whole; the wise silence; the universal beauty, to which every part and particle is equally related; the eternal ONE.

This deep power in which we exist, and whose beatitude is all accessible to us, is not only self-sufficing and perfect in every hour, but the act of seeing and the thing seen, the seer and the spectacle, the subject and the object, are one. We see the world piece by piece, as the sun, the moon, the animal, the tree; but the whole, of which these are the shining parts, is the soul. Only by the vision of that Wisdom can the horoscope of the ages be read, and by falling back on our better thoughts, by yielding to the spirit of prophecy which is innate in every man, we can know what it saith.

I dare not speak for it. My words do not carry its august sense; they fall short and cold. Only itself can inspire whom it will, and, behold! their speech shall be lyrical, and sweet, and universal as the rising of the wind. Yet I desire, even by profane words, if sacred I may not use, to indicate the heaven of this deity, and to report what hints I have collected of the transcendent simplicity and energy of the Highest Law.

A L L   G O E S   T O   S H O W that the soul in man is not an organ, but animates and exercises all the organs; is not a function, like the power of memory, of calcula-tion, of comparison—but uses these as hands and feet; is not a faculty, but a light; is not the intellect or the will, but the master of the intellect and the will; is the vast background of our being, in which they lie—an immensity not possessed and that cannot be possessed. From within or from behind, a light shines through us upon things, and makes us aware that we are nothing, but the light is all. A man is the facade of a temple wherein all wisdom and all good abide.

W H E N   T H E   U N I V E R S A L   S O U L   B R E A T H E S through a man's intellect, it is genius; when it breathes through his will, it is virtue; when it flows through his affection, it is love. And the blindness of the intellect

begins when it would be something of itself. The weakness of the will begins when the individual would be
something of himself. All reform aims, in some one
particular, to let the universal soul have its way
through us; in other words, to engage us to obey.

TO THE SOUL in her pure action all the virtues are
natural, and not painfully acquired. Speak to his heart,
and the man suddenly becomes virtuous.

Within the same sentiment is the germ of intellectual growth, which obeys the same law. Those who are
capable of humility, of justice, of love, of aspiration,
are already on a platform that commands the sciences
and arts, speech and poetry, action and grace. For
whoso dwells in this moral beatitude does already anticipate those special powers which men prize so
highly; just as love does justice to all the gifts of the
object beloved.

The heart which abandons itself to the Supreme
Mind finds itself related to all its works, and will travel
a royal road to particular knowledges and powers. In
ascending to this primary and aboriginal sentiment, we
have come from our remote station on the circumference instantaneously to the center of the world, where,
as in the closet of God, we see causes, and anticipate
the universe, which is but a slow effect.

One mode of the divine teaching is the incarnation

of the spirit in a form—in forms like my own. I live in society; with persons who answer to thoughts in my own mind, or express a certain obedience to the great instincts *[according]* to which I live. I see its presence in them. I am certified of a common nature; and so these other souls, these separated selves, draw me as nothing else can. They stir in me the new emotions we call passion; of love, hatred, fear, admiration, pity; thence comes conversation, competition, persuasion, cities, and war.

IN ALL CONVERSATION between two persons, tacit reference is made as to a third party, to a common nature. That third party or common nature is not social; it is impersonal, is God. And so in groups where debate is earnest, and especially on high questions, the company become aware that the thought rises to an equal level in all bosoms, that all have a spiritual property in what was said, as well as the sayer. They all become wiser than they were. It arches over them like a temple, this unity of thought, in which every heart beats with nobler sense of power and duty, and thinks and acts with unusual solemnity. All are conscious of attaining to a higher self-possession. It shines for all.

There is a certain wisdom of humanity which is common to the greatest men with the lowest, and which our ordinary education often labors to silence and obstruct. The mind is one; and the best minds, who love truth for its own sake, think much less of property in truth *[of owning truth]*. Thankfully they accept it everywhere, and do not label or stamp it with any man's name, for it is theirs long beforehand. It is theirs from eternity.

The learned and the studious of thought have no monopoly on wisdom. Their violence of direction in some degree disqualifies them to think truly. We owe many valuable observations to people who are not very acute or profound, and who say the thing without effort, which we want and have long been hunting in vain. The action of the soul is oftener in that which is felt and left unsaid, than in that which is said in any conversation. It broods over every society, and they unconsciously seek for it in each other. We know better than we do. We do not yet possess ourselves, and we know at the same time that we are much more. I feel the same truth how often in my trivial conversation with my neighbors, that something higher in each of us overlooks this by-play, and Jove nods to Jove from behind each of us.

WE ARE WISER THAN WE KNOW. If we will not interfere with our thought, but will act entirely, or see how the thing stands in God, we know the particular thing, and every thing, and every man. For the Maker of all things and all persons stands behind us, and casts his dread omniscience through us over things.

THERE IS A DIFFERENCE between one and another hour of life in their authority and subsequent effect. Our faith comes in moments; our vice is habitual. Yet is there a depth in those brief moments which constrains us to ascribe more reality to them than to all other experiences.

WE DISTINGUISH THE ANNOUNCEMENTS of the soul, its manifestations of its own nature, by the term *Revelation*. These are always attended by the emotion of the sublime. For this communication is an influx of the Divine mind into our mind. It is an ebb of the individual rivulet before the flowing surges of the sea of life. Every distinct apprehension of this central commandment agitates men with awe and delight. A thrill passes through all men at the reception of new truth, or at the performance of a great action, which comes out of the heart of nature.

In these communications, the power to see is not separated from the will to do, but the insight proceeds from obedience, and the obedience proceeds from a joyful perception. Every moment when the individual feels himself invaded by it is memorable. By the necessity of our constitution, a certain enthusiasm attends the individual's consciousness of that divine presence. The character and duration of this enthusiasm varies with the state of the individual, from an ecstasy and trance and prophetic inspiration — which is its rarer appearance — to the faintest glow of virtuous emotion, in which form it warms, like our household fires, all the families and associations of men, and makes society possible.

I T I S N O T in an arbitrary "decree of God," but in the nature of man, that a veil shuts down on the facts of tomorrow: for the soul will not have us read any other cipher than that of cause and effect. By this veil, which curtains events, it instructs the children of men to live in today. The only mode of obtaining an answer to these questions of the senses is to forego all low curiosity, and, accepting the tide of being which floats us into the secret of nature, work and live, work and live, and all unawares the advancing soul has built and forged for itself a new condition, and the question and the answer are one.

Thus is the soul the perceiver and revealer of truth. By the same fire, vital, consecrating, celestial, which burns until it shall dissolve all things into the waves and surges of an ocean of light—we see and know each other, and what spirit each is of.

By virtue of this inevitable nature, private will is overpowered, and, maugre *[i.e., in spite of]* our efforts or our imperfections, your genius will speak from you, and mine from me. That which we are, we shall teach, not voluntarily, but involuntarily. Thoughts come into our minds by avenues which we never left open, and thoughts go out of our minds through avenues which we never voluntarily opened. Character teaches over our head. The infallible index of true progress is found in the tone the man takes. Neither his age, nor his breeding, nor company, nor books, nor actions, nor talents, nor all together, can hinder him from being deferential to a higher spirit than his own. If he have not found his home in God, his manners, his forms of speech, the turn of his sentences, the build, shall I say, of all his opinions, will involuntarily confess it, let him brave it out how he will. If he have found his center, the Deity will shine through him, through all the disguises of ignorance, of ungenial temperament, of unfavorable circumstance. The tone of seeking is one, and the tone of having is another.

The great distinction between men of the world

who are reckoned accomplished talkers, and here and there a fervent mystic, prophesying half-insane under the infinitude of his thought, is, that one class speak *from within,* or from experience, as parties and possessors of the fact; and the other class, *from without,* as spectators merely, or perhaps as acquainted with the fact on the evidence of third persons. It is of no use to preach to me from without. I can do that too easily myself. Jesus speaks always from within, and in a degree that transcends all others. In that is the miracle.

MUCH OF THE WISDOM of the world is not wisdom, and the most illuminated class of men are no doubt superior to literary fame, and are not writers. Among the multitude of scholars and authors we feel no hallowing presence; we are sensible of a knack and skill rather than of inspiration; they have a light, and know not whence it comes, and call it their own; their talent is some exaggerated faculty, some overgrown member, so that their strength is a disease. In these instances the intellectual gifts do not make the impression of virtue, but almost of vice; and we feel that a man's talents stand in the way of his advancement in truth. But genius is religious. It is a larger imbibing of the common heart. It is not anomalous, but more like, and not less like, other men. There is in all great poets a wisdom of humanity, which is superior to any talents they exercise. The author, the wit, the partisan, the fine gentleman, does not take the place of the man.

THE SOUL THAT ASCENDS to worship the great God is plain and true; has no rose color, no fine friends, no chivalry, no adventures; does not want admiration; dwells in the hour that now is, in the earnest experience of the common day—by reason of the present moment and the mere trifle having become porous to thought, and bibulous of the sea of light.

INEFFABLE IS THE UNION of man and God in every act of the soul. The simplest person who in his integrity worships God becomes God.

WHEN WE HAVE BROKEN our god of tradition, and ceased from our god of rhetoric, then may God fire the heart with his presence. It is the doubling of the heart itself, nay, the infinite enlargement of the heart with a power of growth to a new infinity on every side. It inspires in man an infallible trust. He has not the conviction, but the sight that the best is the true, and may in that thought easily dismiss all particular uncertainties and fears, and adjourn to the sure revelation of time the solution of his private riddles. He is sure that his welfare is dear to the heart of being. In the presence of law to his mind, he is overflowed with a reliance so universal, that it sweeps away all cherished hopes and the most stable projects of mortal condition in its flood. He believes that he cannot escape from his good.

The things that are really for thee gravitate to thee. You are running to seek your friend. Let your feet run, but your mind need not. If you do not find him, will you not acquiesce that it is best you should not find him? For there is a power, which, as it is in you, is in him also, and could therefore very well bring you together, if it were for the best.

You are preparing with eagerness to go and render a service to which your talent and your taste invite you, the love of men and the hope of fame. Has it not occurred to you that you have no right to go unless you are equally willing to be prevented from going?

O believe, as thou livest, that every sound that is spoken over the round world, which thou oughtest to hear, will vibrate on thine ear. Every proverb, every book, every by-word that belongs to thee for aid or comfort, shall surely come home through open or winding passages. Every friend whom not thy fantastic will, but the great and tender heart in thee craveth, shall lock thee in his embrace. And this, because the heart in thee is the heart of all; not a valve, not a wall, not an intersection is there anywhere in nature, but one blood rolls uninterruptedly, an endless circulation, through all men, as the water of the globe is all one sea, and, truly seen, its tide is one.

Let man, then, learn the revelation of all nature, and all thought to his heart; this, namely, that the Highest dwells with him, that the sources of nature are in his own mind, if the sentiment of duty is there. But if he would know what the great God speaketh, he must "go into his closet and shut the door," as Jesus said. God will not make himself manifest to cowards. He must greatly listen to himself, withdrawing himself from all the accents of other men's devotion.

IT MAKES NO DIFFERENCE whether the appeal is to numbers or to one. The faith that stands on authority is not faith. The reliance on authority measures the decline of religion, the withdrawal of the soul. The position men have given to Jesus now for many centuries of history is a position of authority. It characterizes themselves. It cannot alter the eternal facts. Great is the soul, and plain. It is no flatterer, it is no follower; it never appeals from itself. It believes in itself. Before the immense possibilities of man, all mere experience, all past biography, however spotless and sainted, shrinks away.

Before that heaven which our presentiments foreshow us, we cannot easily praise any form of life we have seen or read of. We not only affirm that we have few great men, but, absolutely speaking, that we have none; that we have no history, no record of any character or mode of living that entirely contents us. The saints and demigods whom history worships, we are constrained to accept with a grain of allowance. Though in our lonely hours we draw a new strength out of their memory, yet, pressed on our attention, as they are by the thoughtless and customary, they fatigue and invade.

The soul gives itself, alone, original, and pure, to the Lonely, Original, and Pure, who, on that condition, gladly inhabits, leads, and speaks through it. Then it is glad, young, and nimble. It is not wise, but it sees through all things. It is not called religious, but it is innocent. It calls the light its own, and feels that the grass grows and the stone falls by a law inferior to, and dependent on, its nature.

Behold, it saith, I am born into the great, the universal mind. I, the imperfect, adore my own Perfect. I am somehow receptive of the great soul, and thereby I do overlook [*i.e., look down upon*] the sun and the stars, and feel them to be but the fair accidents and effects which change and pass. More and more the surges of everlasting nature enter into me, and I become public and human in my regards and actions. So I come to live in thoughts, and act with energies, which are immortal.

Thus revering the soul, and learning, as the ancient said, that "its beauty is immense," man will come to see that the world is the perennial miracle which the soul worketh, and be less astonished at particular wonders; he will learn that there is no profane history; that all history is sacred; that the universe is represented in an atom, in a moment of time.

He will weave no longer a spotted life of shreds and patches, but he will live with a divine unity. He will cease from what is base and frivolous in his life, and be content with all places and with any service he can render. He will calmly front the morrow in the negligency of that trust which carries God with it, and so hath already the whole future in the bottom of the heart.

Self-Reliance

TO BELIEVE YOUR OWN THOUGHT, to believe that what is true for you in your private heart is true for all men—that is genius. Speak your latent conviction, and it shall be the universal sense; for the inmost in due time becomes the outmost—and our first thought is rendered back to us by the trumpets of the Last Judgment.

A man should learn to detect and watch that gleam of light which flashes across his mind from within, more than the luster of the firmament of bards and sages. Yet he dismisses without notice his thought, because it is his.

In every work of genius we recognize our own rejected thoughts: they come back to us with a certain alienated majesty. Great works of art have no more affecting lesson for us than this. They teach us to abide by our spontaneous impression with good-humored inflexibility then most when the whole cry of voices is on the other side. Else, tomorrow a stranger will say with masterly good sense precisely what we have thought and felt all the time, and we shall be forced to take with shame our own opinion from another.

THERE IS A TIME in every man's education when he arrives at the conviction that envy is ignorance; that imitation is suicide; that he must take himself for better, for worse, as his portion; that though the wide universe is full of good, no kernel of nourishing corn can come to him but through his toil bestowed on that plot of ground which is given him to till. The power which resides in him is new in nature, and none but he knows what that is which he can do, nor does he know until he has tried. Not for nothing one face, one character, one fact makes much impression on him, and another none.

Trust thyself: every heart vibrates to that iron string. Accept the place the divine providence has found for you, the society of your contemporaries, the connection of events. Great men have always done so, and confided themselves childlike to the genius of their age.

THE MAN IS, as it were, clapped into jail by his consciousness. As soon as he has once acted or spoken with éclat, he is a committed person, watched by the sympathy or the hatred of hundreds, whose affections must now enter into his account. There is no Lethe for this. Ah, that he could pass again into his neutrality! Who can thus avoid all pledges, and having observed, observe again from the same unaffected, unbiased, unbribable, unaffrighted innocence, must always be formidable.

A foolish consistency is the hobgoblin of little minds, adored by little statesmen and philosophers and divines. If you would be a man, speak today what you think today in words as hard as cannon-balls, and tomorrow speak what tomorrow thinks in hard words again, though it contradict everything you said today.

THE VOICES WHICH WE HEAR in solitude grow faint and inaudible as we enter into the world. Society everywhere is in conspiracy against the manhood of every one of its members. Society is a joint-stock company, in which the members agree, for the better securing of his bread to each shareholder, to surrender the liberty and culture of the eater. The virtue in most request is conformity. Self-reliance is its aversion. It loves not realities and creators, but names and customs.

Whoso would be a man must be a nonconformist. He who would gather immortal palms must not be hindered by the name of goodness, but must explore if it be goodness. Nothing is at last sacred but the integrity of our own mind. Absolve you to yourself, and you shall have the suffrage of the world.

TRUTH IS HANDSOMER than the affectation of love. Your goodness must have some edge to it—else it is none.

I DO NOT WISH TO EXPIATE, but to live. My life is for itself and not for a spectacle.

What I must do is all that concerns me, not what the people think. This rule, equally arduous in actual and in intellectual life, may serve for the whole distinction between greatness and meanness. It is the harder, because you will always find those who think they know what is your duty better than you know it. It is easy in the world to live after the world's opinion; it is easy in solitude to live after our own; but the great man is he who in the midst of the crowd keeps with perfect sweetness the independence of solitude.

THE MAGNETISM which all original action exerts is explained when we inquire the reason of self-trust. Who is the Trustee? What is the aboriginal Self on which a universal reliance may be grounded? What is the nature and power of that science-baffling star, without parallax, without calculable elements, which shoots a ray of beauty even into trivial and impure actions, if the least mark of independence appear?

The inquiry leads us to that source, at once the essence of genius, the essence of virtue, and the essence of life, which we call Spontaneity or Instinct. We denote this primary wisdom as Intuition, whilst all later teachings are tuitions. In that deep force, the last fact, behind which analysis cannot go, all things find their common origin. For the sense of being, which in calm hours rises, we know not how, in the soul, is not diverse from things, from space, from light, from time, from man, but one with them, and proceeds obviously from the same source whence their life and being also proceed.

We first share the life by which things exist, and afterwards see them as appearances in nature, and forget that we have shared their cause. Here is the fountain of action and of thought. Here are the lungs of that inspiration which giveth man wisdom, of that inspiration of man which cannot be denied without impiety and atheism.

We lie in the lap of immense intelligence, which

makes us receivers of its truth and organs of its activity. When we discern justice, when we discern truth, we do nothing of ourselves but allow a passage to its beams. If we ask whence this comes, if we seek to pry into the soul that causes, all philosophy is at fault. Its presence or its absence is all we can affirm.

WHENCE, THEN, THIS WORSHIP of the past? The centuries are conspirators against the sanity and authority of the soul. Time and space are but physiological colors which the eye makes, but the soul is light; where it is, is day; where it was, is night; and history is an impertinence and an injury if it be anything more than a cheerful apologue or parable of my being and becoming.

Man is timid and apologetic. He is no longer upright. He dares not say, "I think," "I am," but quotes some saint or sage. He is ashamed before the blade of grass or the blowing rose. These roses under my window make no reference to former roses or to better ones; they are for what they are; they exist with God today. There is no time to them. There is simply the rose; it is perfect in every moment of its existence.

But man postpones or remembers; he does not live in the present, but with reverted eye laments the past, or, heedless of the riches that surround him, stands on tiptoe to foresee the future. He cannot be happy and strong until he too lives with nature in the present, above time. When a man lives with God, his voice shall be as sweet as the murmur of the brook and the rustle of the corn.

WHEN GOOD IS NEAR YOU, when you have life in yourself, it is not by any known or accustomed way; you shall not discern the footprints of any other; you shall not see the face of man; you shall not hear any name; the way, the thought, the good, shall be wholly strange and new. It shall exclude example and experience. Fear and hope are alike beneath it. There is something low even in hope. In the hour of vision, there is nothing that can be called gratitude, nor properly joy. The soul raised over passion beholds identity and eternal causation, perceives the self-existence of Truth and Right, and calms itself with knowing that all things go well.

ONLY LIFE AVAILS, not the having lived. Power ceases in the instant of repose; it resides in the moment of transition from a past to a new state, in the shooting of the gulf, in the darting to an aim. This one fact the world hates, that the soul *becomes;* for that forever degrades the past, turns all riches to poverty, all reputation to a shame, confounds the saint with the rogue, shoves Jesus and Judas equally aside.

WE DO NOT YET SEE that virtue is Height, and that a man or a company of men plastic and permeable to principles, by the law of nature must overpower and ride all cities, nations, kings, rich men, poets, who are not. This is the ultimate fact which we so quickly reach on this as on every topic, the resolution of all into the ever-blessed ONE. Self-existence is the attribute of the Supreme Cause, and it constitutes the measure of good by the degree in which it enters into all lower forms. All things real are so by so much virtue as they contain.

Thus all concentrates: let us not rove; let us sit at home with the cause. Let us stun and astonish the intruding rabble of men and books and institutions by a simple declaration of the divine fact. Bid the invaders take the shoes from off their feet, for God is here within. Let our simplicity judge them, and our docility to our own law demonstrate the poverty of nature and fortune beside our native riches.

WE MUST GO ALONE. Isolation must precede true society. But your isolation must not be mechanical, but spiritual, that is, must be elevation. At times the whole world seems to be in conspiracy to importune you with emphatic trifles. Friend, client, child, sickness, fear, want, charity, all knock at once at thy closet-door and say, "Come out unto us." But keep thy state; come not into their confusion. The power men possess to annoy me, I give them by a weak curiosity. No man can come near me but through my act.

I MUST BE MYSELF. I cannot break myself any longer for you, or you. If you can love me for what I am, we shall be the happier. If you cannot, I will still seek to deserve that you should. I will not hide my tastes or aversions. I will so trust that what is deep is holy, that I will do strongly before the sun and moon whatever inly rejoices me, and the heart appoints. If you are noble, I will love you; if you are not, I will not hurt you and myself by hypocritical attentions. If you are true, but not in the same truth with me, cleave to your companions; I will seek my own. I do this not selfishly, but humbly and truly. It is alike your interest and mine and all men's, however long we have dwelt in lies, to live in truth. Does this sound harsh today? You will soon love what is dictated by your nature as well as mine; and if we follow the truth, it will bring us out safe at last.

But so you may give these friends pain. Yes, but I cannot sell my liberty and my power to save their sensibility. Besides, all persons have their moments of reason, when they look out into the region of absolute truth; then they will justify me and do the same thing.

THE POPULACE THINK that your rejection of popular standards is a rejection of all standard, and mere antinomianism; and the bold sensualist will use the name of philosophy to gild his crimes. But the law of consciousness abides.

Truly it demands something godlike in him who has cast off the common motives of humanity, and has ventured to trust himself for a taskmaster. High be his heart, faithful his will, clear his sight, that he may in good earnest be doctrine, society, law to himself, that a simple purpose may be to him as strong as iron necessity is to others!

IF OUR YOUNG MEN MISCARRY in their first enterprises, they lose all heart. If the young merchant fails, men say he is *ruined*. If the finest genius studies at one of our colleges, and is not installed in an office within one year afterwards in the cities or suburbs of Boston or New York, it seems to his friends and to himself that he is right in being disheartened and in complaining the rest of his life. A sturdy lad from New Hampshire or Vermont, who in turn tries all the professions, who teams it, farms it, peddles, keeps a school, preaches, edits a newspaper, goes to Congress, buys a township, and so forth, in successive years, and always, like a cat, falls on his feet, is worth a hundred of these city dolls. He walks abreast with his days, and feels no shame in not "studying a profession," for he does not postpone his life, but lives already. He has not one chance, but a hundred chances.

LET A STOIC ARISE who shall reveal the resources of man, and tell men they are not leaning willows, but can and must detach themselves; that with the exercise of self-trust, new powers shall appear; that a man is the word made flesh, born to shed healing to the nations; that he should be ashamed of our compassion; and that the moment he acts from himself, tossing the laws, the books, idolatries, and customs out of the window, we pity him no more, but thank and revere him. That teacher shall restore the life of man to splendor, and make his name dear to all history.

PRAYER THAT CRAVES a particular commodity—anything less than all good—is vicious. Prayer is the contemplation of the facts of life from the highest point of view. It is the soliloquy of a beholding and jubilant soul. It is the spirit of God pronouncing his works good. But prayer as a means to effect a private end is theft and meanness. It supposes dualism and not unity in nature and consciousness. As soon as the man is at one with God, he will not beg.

ANOTHER SORT OF FALSE PRAYERS are our regrets. Discontent is the want of self-reliance: it is infirmity of will. Regret calamities if you can thereby help the sufferer; if not, attend your own work, and already the evil begins to be repaired. Our sympathy is just as base. We come to them who weep foolishly, and sit down and cry for company, instead of imparting to them truth and health in rough electric shocks, putting them once more in communication with their own reason.

The secret of fortune is joy in our hands. Welcome evermore to gods and men is the self-helping man. For him all doors are flung wide. Him all tongues greet, all honors crown, all eyes follow with desire. Our love goes out to him and embraces him, because he did not need it.

THE SOUL IS NO TRAVELLER; the wise man stays at home, and when his necessities, his duties, on any occasion call him from his house, or into foreign lands, he is at home still, and shall make men sensible by the expression of his countenance that he goes the missionary of wisdom and virtue, and visits cities and men like a sovereign, and not like an interloper or a valet.

Travelling is a fool's paradise. Our first journeys discover to us the indifference of places. At home I dream that at Naples, at Rome, I can be intoxicated with beauty, and lose my sadness. I pack my trunk, embrace my friends, embark on the sea, and at last wake up in Naples, and there beside me is the stern fact, the sad self, unrelenting, identical, that I fled from.

But the rage of travelling is a symptom of a deeper

unsoundness, affecting the whole intellectual action. The intellect is vagabond, and the universal system of education fosters restlessness. Our minds travel when our bodies are forced to stay at home. We imitate; and what is imitation but the travelling of the mind?

The soul created the arts wherever they have flourished. It was in his own mind that the artist sought his model. It was an application of his own thought to the thing to be done and the conditions to be observed.

Insist on yourself; never imitate. Your own gift you can present every moment with the cumulative force of a whole life's cultivation; but of the adopted talent of another you have only an extemporaneous, half possession.

SOCIETY NEVER ADVANCES. It recedes as fast on one side as it gains on the other. It undergoes continual changes; it is barbarous, it is civilized, it is christianized, it is rich, it is scientific; but this change is not amelioration. For every thing that is given, something is taken. Society acquires new arts, and loses old instincts.

THE RELIANCE ON PROPERTY, including the reliance on governments which protect it, is the want of self-reliance. Men have looked away from themselves and at things so long that they have come to esteem the religious, learned, and civil institutions as guards of property, and they deprecate assaults on these, because they feel them to be assaults on property. They measure their esteem of each other by what each has, and not by what each is. But a cultivated man becomes ashamed of his property, out of new respect for his being. Especially he hates what he has, if he see that it is accidental—came to him by inheritance, or gift, or crime; then he feels that it is not having; it does not belong to him, has no root in him, and merely lies there because no revolution or no robber takes it away.

HE WHO KNOWS THAT POWER IS INBORN, that he is weak because he has looked for good outside of himself and elsewhere, and so perceiving, throws himself unhesitatingly on his thought, instantly rights himself, stands in the erect position, commands his limbs, works miracles; just as a man who stands on his feet is stronger than a man who stands on his head.

So use all that is called Fortune. Most men gamble with her, and gain all, or lose all, as her wheel rolls.

But do thou leave as unlawful these winnings, and deal with Cause and Effect, the chancellors of God. In the Will work and acquire, and thou hast chained the wheel of Chance, and shalt sit hereafter without fear of her rotations. A political victory, a rise of rents, the recovery of your sick, or the return of your absent friend, or some other quite external event, raises your spirits, and you think good days are preparing for you. Do not believe it. Nothing can bring you peace but yourself. Nothing can bring you peace but the triumph of principles.

Compensation

EVER SINCE I WAS A BOY, I have wished to write a discourse on Compensation: for it seemed to me when very young, that on this subject life was ahead of theology, and the people knew more than the preachers taught. I was lately confirmed in these desires by hearing a sermon at church. The preacher, a man esteemed for his orthodoxy, unfolded in the ordinary manner the doctrine of the Last Judgment. He assumed that judgment is not executed in this world; that the wicked are successful; that the good are miserable; and then urged from reason and from Scripture a compensation to be made to both parties in the next life.

Yet what was the import of this teaching? What did the preacher mean by saying that the good are miserable in the present life? Was it that houses and lands, offices, wine, horses, dress, luxury, are had by

unprincipled men, whilst the saints are poor and de-
spised; and that a compensation is to be made to these
last hereafter, by giving them the like gratifications
another day—bank-stock and doubloons, venison and
champagne? This must be the compensation intended;
for what else? Is it that they are to have leave to pray
and praise? to love and serve men? Why, that they can
do now. The legitimate inference the disciple would
draw, was: "We are to have *such* a good time as the
sinners have now"—or, to push it to its extreme import: "You sin now; we shall sin by and by: we would
sin now, if we could; not being successful, we expect
our revenge tomorrow."

The fallacy lay in the immense concession that
the bad are successful; that justice is not done now.
The blindness of the preacher consisted in deferring
to the base estimate of the market of what constitutes
a manly success, instead of confronting and convicting
the world from the truth; announcing the presence of
the soul, the omnipotence of the will; and so establish-
ing the standard of good and ill, of success and falsehood.

POLARITY, OR ACTION AND REACTION,
we meet in every part of nature; in darkness and light;
in heat and cold; in the ebb and flow of waters; in male

and female; in the inspiration and expiration of plants
and animals; in the systole and diastole of the heart.
Whilst the world is thus dual, so is every one of its
parts. The entire system of things gets represented in
every particle.

The same dualism underlies the nature and condition of man. Every excess causes a defect; every
defect an excess. Every sweet hath its sour; every evil
its good. Every faculty which is a receiver of pleasure,
has an equal penalty on its abuse. It is to answer for its
moderation with its life. For every grain of wit there is
a grain of folly. For every thing you have missed, you
have gained something else; and for every thing you
gain, you lose something.

The farmer imagines power and place are fine
things. But the President has paid dear for his White
House. It has commonly cost him all his peace and the
best of his manly attributes. To preserve for a short
time so conspicuous an appearance before the world,
he is content to eat dust before the real masters, who
stand erect behind the throne.

This law writes the laws of cities and nations. It is
in vain to build or plot or combine against it. Things
refuse to be mismanaged long. Though no checks to a
new evil appear, the checks exist, and will appear. If
the government is cruel, the governor's life is not safe.
If you tax too high, the revenue will yield nothing. If
you make the criminal code sanguinary, juries will not
convict. Nothing arbitrary, nothing artificial can endure. The true life and satisfactions of man seem to

elude the utmost rigors or felicities of condition, and to establish themselves with great indifference under all varieties of circumstance.

These appearances indicate the fact that the universe is represented in every one of its particles. Every thing in nature contains all the powers of nature. Every thing is made of one hidden stuff; as the naturalist sees one type under every metamorphosis. Each new form repeats not only the main character of the type, but part for part all the details, all the aims, furtherances, hindrances, energies, and whole system of every other. Every occupation, trade, art, transaction, is a compend of the world, and a correlative of every other. Each one is an entire emblem of human life: of its good and ill, its trials, its enemies, its course, and its end. And each one must somehow accommodate the whole man, and recite all his destiny.

Thus is the universe alive. All things are moral. That soul which within us is a sentiment, outside of us is a law. We feel its inspiration; out there in history we can see its fatal strength. It is almighty. All nature feels its grasp. It is eternal, but it enacts itself in time and space. Justice is not postponed. A perfect equity adjusts its balance in all parts of life. The dice of God are always loaded. The world looks like a multiplication table or a mathematical equation, which, turn it how you will, balances itself.

EVERY SECRET IS TOLD, every crime is punished, every virtue rewarded, every wrong redressed,
in silence and certainty. Every act rewards itself.

The specific stripes may follow late after the of-
fence, but they follow because they accompany it.
Crime and punishment grow out of one stem. Punishment is a fruit that unsuspected ripens within the
flower of the pleasure which concealed it. Cause and
effect, means and ends, seed and fruit, cannot be sev-
ered; for the effect already blooms in the cause, the
end pre-exists in the means, the fruit in the seed.

Whilst thus the world will be whole, and refuses
to be disparted, we seek to act partially, to sunder, to
appropriate. For example, to gratify the senses we
sever the pleasure of the senses from the needs of the
character. The ingenuity of man has been dedicated
always to the solution of one problem—how to detach
the sensual sweet, the sensual strong, the sensual
bright, etc., from the moral sweet, the moral deep, the
moral fair; that is, again, to contrive to get a *one end*,
without an *other end*. The soul says, Eat; the body
would feast. The soul says, The man and woman shall
be one flesh and one soul; the body would join the
flesh only. The soul says, Have dominion over all
things to the ends of virtue; the body would have the
power over things to its own ends.

Life invests itself with inevitable conditions, which
the unwise seek to dodge, which one and another brags
that he does not know; brags that they do not touch
him; but the brag is on his lips, the conditions are in his

soul. If he escapes them in one part, they attack him in another more vital part. If he has escaped them in form and in the appearance, it is that he has resisted his life and fled from himself; and the retribution is so much death.

You cannot do wrong without suffering wrong. "No man had ever a point of pride that was not injurious to him," said Burke. The exclusive in fashionable life does not see that he excludes himself from enjoyment, in the attempt to appropriate it. The exclusionist in religion does not see that he shuts the door of heaven on himself, in striving to shut out others.

All infractions of love and equity in our social relations are speedily punished. They are punished by fear. Whilst I stand in simple relations to my fellow man, I have no displeasure in meeting him.

All the old abuses in society, universal and particular, all unjust accumulations of property and power, are avenged in the same manner. Fear is an instructor of great sagacity, and the herald of all revolutions.

Experienced men of the world know very well that it is always best to pay scot and lot as they go along, and that a man often pays dear for a small frugality. Has a man gained any thing who has received a hundred favors and rendered none? He may soon come to see that "the highest price he can pay for a thing is to ask for it."

A wise man will extend this lesson to all parts of life, and know that it is always the part of prudence to face every claimant, and pay every just demand on your time, your talents, or your heart.

THE GOOD ARE BEFRIENDED even by weakness and defect. As no man ever had a point of pride that was not injurious to him, so no man had ever a defect that was not somewhere made useful to him.

Has he a defect of temper that unfits him to live in society? Thereby he is driven to entertain himself alone, and acquire habits of self-help; and thus, like the wounded oyster, he mends his shell with pearl.

Our strength grows out of our weakness. The indignation which arms itself with secret forces does not awaken until we are pricked and stung and sorely assailed. A great man is always willing to be little. Whilst he sits on the cushion of advantages, he goes to sleep. When he is pushed, tormented, defeated, he has a chance to learn something; he has been put on his wits, on his manhood; he has gained facts; learns his ignorance; is cured of the insanity of conceit; has got moderation and real skill.

The wise man throws himself on the side of his assailants. It is more his interest than it is theirs to find his weak point. Blame is safer than praise. I hate to be defended in a newspaper. As long as all that is said is said against me, I feel a certain assurance of success.

But as soon as honeyed words of praise are spoken for me, I feel as one that lies unprotected before his enemies. In general, every evil to which we do not succumb is a benefactor. As the Sandwich Islander believes that the strength and valor of the enemy he kills passes into himself, so we gain the strength of the temptation we resist.

IN A VIRTUOUS ACTION, I properly *am;* in a virtuous act, I add to the world; I plant into deserts conquered from Chaos and Nothing, and see the darkness receding on the limits of the horizon.

I NO LONGER WISH to meet a good I do not earn—for example, to find a pot of buried gold—knowing that it brings with it new responsibility. I do not wish more external goods—neither possessions, nor honors, nor powers, nor persons. The gain is apparent, the tax is certain. But there is no tax on the knowledge that the compensation exists, and that it is not desirable to dig up treasure. Herein I rejoice with a serene eternal peace. I contract the boundaries of possible mischief. I learn the wisdom of St. Bernard: "Nothing can work me damage except myself; the harm that I sustain, I carry about with me, and never am a real sufferer but by my own fault."

SUCH, ALSO, IS THE NATURAL HISTORY of calamity. The changes which break up at short intervals the prosperity of men are advertisements of a nature whose law is growth. Every soul is by this intrinsic necessity quitting its whole system of things, its friends, and home, and laws, and faith, as the shell-fish crawls out of its beautiful but stony case, because it no longer admits of its growth, and slowly forms a new house. In proportion to the vigor of the individual, these revolutions are frequent, until in some happier mind they are incessant, and all worldly relations hang very loosely about him, becoming, as it were, a transparent fluid membrane through which the living form is seen, and not, as in most men, an indurated heterogeneous fabric of many dates, and of no settled character, in which the man is imprisoned. Then there can be enlargement, and the man of today scarcely recognizes the man of yesterday. Such should be the outward biography of man in time, a putting off of dead circumstances day by day, as he renews his raiment day by day. But to us, in our lapsed estate, resting, not advancing, resisting, not cooperating with the divine expansion, this growth comes by shocks.

We cannot part with our friends. We cannot let our angels go. We do not see that they go out only so that archangels may come in. We are idolaters of the old. We do not believe in the riches of the soul, in its proper eternity and omnipresence. We do not believe there is any force in today to rival or recreate that beautiful yesterday. We linger in the ruins of the old tent, where once we had bread and shelter and organs, nor believe that the spirit can feed, cover, and nerve us again. We cannot again find aught so dear, so sweet, so graceful. But we sit and weep in vain. The voice of the Almighty saith, "Up and onward for evermore!" We cannot stay amid the ruins. Neither will we rely on the new; and so we walk ever with reverted eyes, like those monsters who look backwards.

And yet the compensations of calamity are made apparent to the understanding also, after long intervals of time. A fever, a mutilation, a cruel disappointment, a loss of wealth, a loss of friends, seems at the moment unpaid loss, and unpayable. But the sure years reveal the deep remedial force that underlies all facts. The death of a dear friend, wife, brother, lover, which seemed nothing but privation, somewhat later assumes the aspect of a guide or genius; for it commonly operates revolutions in our way of life, terminates an epoch of infancy or of youth which was waiting to be closed, breaks up a wonted occupation, or a household, or style of living, and allows the formation of new ones more friendly to the growth of character. It permits or constrains the formation of new acquaintances, and the reception of new influences that prove of the first importance to the next years; and the man or woman who would have remained a sunny garden-flower, with no room for its roots and too much sunshine for its head, by the falling of the walls and the neglect of the gardener, is made the banyan of the forest, yielding shade and fruit to wide neighborhoods of men.

History

THERE IS ONE MIND common to all individual men. Every man is an inlet to the same and to all of the same. He that is once admitted to the right of reason is made a freeman of the whole estate. What Plato has thought, he may think; what a saint has felt, he may feel; what at any time has befallen any man, he can understand. Who hath access to this universal mind is a party to all that is or can be done, for this is the only and sovereign agent. Of the works of this mind history is the record.

Man is explicable by nothing less than all his history. Without hurry, without rest, the human spirit goes forth from the beginning to embody every faculty, every thought, every emotion, which belongs to it, in appropriate events. But always the thought is prior to the fact; all the facts of history pre-exist in the mind as laws. Each law in turn is made by circumstances pre-dominant, and the limits of nature give power to but one at a time. A man is the whole encyclopedia of facts. The creation of a thousand forests is in one acorn; and Egypt, Greece, Rome, Gaul, Britain, America, lie folded already in the first man. Epoch after epoch, camp, kingdom, empire, republic, democracy, are merely the application of his manifold nature to the manifold world.

THIS HUMAN MIND WROTE HISTORY, and this must read it. If the whole of history is in one man, it is all to be explained from individual experience. Of the universal mind each individual man is one more incarnation. All its properties consist in him. Each new fact in his private experience flashes a light on what great bodies of men have done, and the crises of his life refer to national crises. Every revolution was first a thought in one man's mind; and when the same thought occurs to another man, it is the key to that era. Every reform was once a private opinion; and when it shall be a private opinion again, it will solve the problem of the age.

The fact narrated must correspond to something in me to be credible or intelligible. We as we read must become Greeks, Romans, Turks, priest and king, martyr and executioner, must fasten these images to some reality in our secret experience, or we shall learn nothing rightly.

IT IS THIS UNIVERSAL NATURE which gives worth to particular men and things. Human life as containing this is mysterious and inviolable, and we hedge it round with penalties and laws. All laws derive hence their ultimate reason; all express more or less distinctly some command of this supreme illimitable essence. Property also holds of the soul, covers great spiritual facts, and instinctively we at first hold to it with swords and laws, and wide and complex combinations. The obscure consciousness of this fact is the light of all our day, the claim of claims; the plea for education, for justice, for charity, the foundation of friendship and love, and of the heroism and grandeur which belongs to acts of self-reliance.

WE SYMPATHIZE in the great moments of history, in the great discoveries, the great resistances, the great prosperities of men—because there law was enacted, the sea was searched, the land was found, or the blow was struck *for us,* as we ourselves in that place would have done or applauded.

The student is to read history actively and not passively; to esteem his own life the text, and books the commentary. Thus compelled, the muse of history will utter oracles, as never to those who do not respect themselves. I have no expectation that any man will read history aright, who thinks that what was done in a remote age, by men whose names have resounded far, has any deeper sense than what he is doing today.

The world exists for the education of each man. There is no age or state of society, or mode of action in history, to which there is not something corresponding in his life.

We are always coming up with the emphatic facts of history in our private experience, and verifying them here. All history becomes subjective; in other words, there is properly no history; only biography *[i.e., autobiography].* Every mind must know the whole lesson for itself—must go over the whole ground. What it does not see, what it does not live, it will not know

ALL INQUIRY into antiquity—all curiosity respecting the pyramids, the excavated cities, Stonehenge, the Ohio Circles, Mexico, Memphis—is the desire to do

away this wild, savage and preposterous There or Then, and introduce in its place the Here and the Now. It is to banish the *Not me* and supply the *Me*. It is to abolish difference, and restore unity! Belzoni digs and measures in the mummy-pits and pyramids of Thebes, until he can see the end of the difference between the monstrous work and himself. When he has satisfied himself, in general and in detail, that it was made by such a person as himself, so armed and so motivated, and to ends to which he himself in given circumstances should also have worked, the problem is then solved; his thought lives along the whole line of temples and sphinxes and catacombs, passes through them all, with satisfaction, and they live again to the mind, or are *now*.

THE DIFFERENCE BETWEEN MEN is in their principle of association. Some men classify objects by color and size and other accidents of appearance; others by intrinsic likeness, or by the relation of cause and effect. The progress of the intellect is to the clearer vision of causes, which neglects surface differences. To the poet, to the philosopher, to the saint, all things are friendly and sacred, all events profitable, all days holy, all men divine. For the eye is fastened on life, and slights the circumstance. Every chemical substance, every plant, every animal in its growth, teaches the unity of cause, the variety of appearance. Genius studies the casual thought, and, far back in the womb of things, sees the rays parting from one orb, that diverge ere they fall by infinite diameters. Genius watches the monad through all his masks as he performs the metempsychosis of nature. *[i.e., Genius sees the unity of the divine soul behind all the variety of nature.]*

The identity of history is equally intrinsic, the diversity equally obvious. There is at the surface infinite variety of things; at the center there is simplicity of cause.

IT IS THE SPIRIT and not the fact that is identical. By descending far down into the depths of the soul, and not primarily by a painful acquisition of many manual skills, the artist attains the power of awakening other souls to a given activity.

Civil and natural history, the history of art and of literature—all must be explained from individual history, or must remain words. There is nothing but is related to us, nothing that does not interest us—kingdom, college, tree, horse, or iron shoe. The roots of all things are in man. The true poem is the poet's mind; the true ship is the ship-builder. In the man, could we lay him open, we should see the sufficient reason for the last flourish and tendril of his work, as every spine and tint in the seashell pre-exist in the secreting organs of the fish.

EVERY THING THE INDIVIDUAL SEES without him *[i.e., outside himself]* corresponds to his states of mind, and every thing is in turn intelligible to him, as his onward thinking leads him into the truth to which that fact or series belongs.

What is the foundation of that interest all men feel in Greek history, letters, art, and poetry, in all its periods, from the heroic or Homeric age, down to the domestic life of the Athenians and Spartans, four or five centuries later? What but this, that every man passes personally through a Grecian period. The Grecian state is the era of the bodily nature, the perfection of the senses—of the spiritual nature unfolded in strict unity with the body. In it existed those human forms which supplied the sculptor with his models of Hercules, Phoebus, and Jove; not like the forms abounding in the streets of modern cities, wherein the face is a confused blur of features, but composed of incorrupt, sharply defined and symmetrical features, whose eye-sockets are so formed that it would be impossible for such eyes to squint, and take furtive glances on this side and on that, but they must turn the whole head.

The manners of that period are plain and fierce. The reverence exhibited is for personal qualities, courage, address, self-command, justice, strength, swiftness, a loud voice, a broad chest. Luxury and elegance are not known. A sparse population and want make every man his own valet, cook, butcher, and soldier; and the habit of supplying his own needs educates the body to wonderful performances.

The costly charm of the ancient tragedy, and indeed of all the old literature, is that the persons speak simply—speak as persons who have great good sense without knowing it, before yet the reflective habit has become the predominant habit of the mind. Our admiration of the antique is not admiration of the old, but of the natural.

NEAR AND PROPER TO US is that old fable of the Sphinx, who was said to sit in the roadside and put riddles to every passenger. If the man could not answer, she swallowed him alive. If he could solve the riddle, the Sphinx was slain. What is our life but an endless flight of winged facts or events? In splendid variety these changes come, all putting questions to the human spirit. Those men who cannot answer by a superior wisdom these facts or questions of time, serve them. Facts encumber them, tyrannize over them, and make the men of routine the men of *sense*, in whom a literal obedience to facts has extinguished every spark of that light by which man is truly man. But if the man is true to his better instincts or sentiments, and refuses the domination of facts, remains fast by the soul and sees the principle, then the facts fall aptly and supple into their places; they know their master, and the meanest of them glorifies him.

A MIND MIGHT PONDER its thought for ages, and not gain so much self-knowledge as the passion of love shall teach it in a day. Who knows himself before he has been thrilled with indignation at an outrage, or has heard an eloquent tongue, or has shared the throb of thousands in a national exultation or alarm? No man can antedate his experience, or guess what faculty or feeling a new object shall unlock, any more than he can draw today the face of a person whom he shall see tomorrow for the first time.

WHAT DOES HISTORY YET RECORD of the metaphysical annals of man? What light does it shed on those mysteries which we hide under the names Death and Immortality? Yet every history should be written in a wisdom which divined the range of our affinities and looked at facts as symbols. I am ashamed to see what a shallow village-tale our so-called History is.

Broader and deeper we must write our annals — from an ethical reformation, from an influx of the ever new, ever sanative conscience — if we would trulier express our central and wide-related nature, instead of this old chronology of selfishness and pride to which we have too long lent our eyes.

Friendship

WE HAVE A GREAT DEAL more kindness than is ever spoken. Maugre *[i.e., in spite of]* all the selfishness that chills like east winds the world, the whole human family is bathed with an element of love like a fine ether. How many persons we meet in houses, whom we scarcely speak to, whom yet we honor, and who honor us! How many we see in the street, or sit with in church, whom, though silently, we warmly rejoice to be with! Read the language of these wandering eye-beams. The heart knoweth.

The effect of the indulgence of this human affection is a certain cordial exhilaration.

MY FRIENDS HAVE COME to me unsought. The great God gave them to me. By oldest right, by the divine affinity of virtue with itself, I find them, or rather not I, but the Deity in me and in them derides and cancels the thick walls of individual character, relation, age, sex, circumstance, at which he usually connives, and now makes many one. High thanks I owe you, excellent lovers, who carry out the world for me to new and noble depths, and enlarge the meaning of all my thoughts.

Yet the systole and diastole of the heart are not without their analogy in the ebb and flow of love. Friendship, like the immortality of the soul, is too good to be believed. In the golden hour of friendship, we are surprised with shades of suspicion and unbelief. We doubt *[i.e., suspect]* that we bestow on our hero the virtues in which he shines, and afterwards worship the form to which we have ascribed this divine inhabitation.

I cannot deny it, O friend, that the vast shadow of the Phenomenal includes thee also in its pied and painted immensity—thee also, compared with whom all else is shadow. Thou art not Being, as Truth is, as Justice is; thou art not my soul, but a picture and effigy of that. Thou hast come to me lately, and already thou art seizing thy hat and cloak. Is it not that the soul puts forth friends as the tree puts forth leaves, and presently, by the germination of new buds, extrudes the old leaf?

The law of nature is alternation for evermore. Each electrical state superinduces the opposite. The soul environs itself with friends, that it may enter into a grander self-acquaintance or solitude; and it goes alone for a season, that it may exalt its conversation or society. This method betrays *[i.e., reveals]* itself along the whole history of our personal relations. The instinct of affection revives the hope of union with our mates, and the returning sense of insulation recalls us from the chase.

OUR FRIENDSHIPS HURRY to short and poor conclusions, because we have made them a texture of wine and dreams, instead of the tough fiber of the human heart. The laws of friendship are austere and eternal, of one web with the laws of nature and of morals. But we have aimed at a swift and petty benefit, to suck a sudden sweetness. We snatch at the slowest fruit in the whole garden of God, which many summers and many winters must ripen. We seek our friend not sacredly, but with an adulterate passion, which would appropriate him to ourselves. In vain. The good spirit of our life has no heaven which is the price *[i.e., the reward]* of rashness.

[Fortunately,] bashfulness and apathy are a tough husk, in which a delicate organization *[i.e., a new friendship]* is protected from premature ripening.

LOVE, which is the essence of God, is not for levity, but for the total worth of man.

I DO NOT WISH to treat friendships daintily, but with roughest courage. When they are real, they are not glass threads or frost-work, but the solidest thing we know. For now, after so many ages of experience, what do we know of nature, or of ourselves? Not one step has man taken toward the solution of the problem of his destiny. In one condemnation of folly stand the whole universe of men. But the sweet sincerity of joy and peace, which I draw from this alliance with my brother's soul, is the nut itself whereof all nature and all thought is but the husk and shell.

THERE ARE TWO ELEMENTS that go to the composition of friendship, each so sovereign, that I can detect no superiority in either, no reason why either should be first named. One is Truth. A friend is a person with whom I may be sincere. Before him I may think aloud. I am arrived at last in the presence of a man so real and equal, that I may drop even those undermost garments of dissimulation, courtesy, and second thought, which men never put off, and may deal with him with the simplicity and wholeness with which one chemical atom meets another. Sincerity is the luxury allowed, like diadems and authority, only to the highest rank, *that* being permitted to speak truth, as having none above it to court or conform unto.

Every man alone is sincere. At the entrance of a second person, hypocrisy begins. We parry and fend the approach of our fellow man by compliments, by gossip, by amusements, by affairs. We cover up our thought from him under a hundred folds.

I knew a man who, under a certain religious frenzy, cast off this drapery, and, omitting all compliment and commonplace, spoke to the conscience of every person he encountered, and that with great insight and beauty. At first he was resisted, and all men agreed he was mad. But persisting, as indeed he could not help doing, for some time in this course, he attained to the advantage of bringing every man of his acquaintance into true relations with him. No man would think of speaking falsely with him, or of putting him off with any chat of markets or reading-rooms. But every man was constrained by so much sincerity to the like plain dealing, and what love of nature, what poetry, what symbol of truth he had, he did certainly show him.

To most of us society shows not its face and eye, but its side and its back. To stand in true relations with men in a false age is worth a fit of insanity, is it not?

We can seldom go erect. Almost every man we meet requires some civility, requires to be humored; he has some fame, some talent, some whim of religion or philanthropy in his head that is not to be questioned, and which spoils all conversation with him. But a friend is a sane man who exercises not my ingenuity, but me. My friend gives me entertainment without requiring any stipulation on my part. A friend, therefore, is a sort of paradox in nature. I who alone am, I who see nothing in nature whose existence I can affirm with equal evidence to my own, behold now the semblance of my being in all its height, variety, and curiosity, reiterated in a foreign form; so that a friend may well be reckoned the masterpiece of nature.

The other element of friendship is tenderness. We are holden to men by every sort of tie, by blood, by pride, by fear, by hope, by lucre, by lust, by hate, by admiration, by every circumstance and badge and trifle, but we can scarce believe that so much character can subsist in another as to draw us by love. Can another be so blessed, and we so pure, that we can offer him tenderness? When a man becomes dear to me, I have touched the goal of fortune.

THE END *[i.e., the goal]* OF FRIENDSHIP is a commerce the most strict and homely that can be joined; more strict than any of which we have experience. It is for aid and comfort through all the relations and passages of life and death. It is fit for serene days, and graceful gifts, and country rambles, but also for rough roads and hard fare, shipwreck, poverty, and persecution. It keeps company with the sallies of wit and the trances of religion. We are to dignify to each other the daily needs and offices of man's life, and embellish it by courage, wisdom, and unity. It should never fall into something usual and settled, but should be alert and inventive, and add rhyme and reason to what was drudgery.

FRIENDSHIP REQUIRES that rare mean betwixt likeness and unlikeness, that piques each with the presence of power and of consent in the other party. Better be a nettle in the side of your friend than his echo. The condition which high friendship demands is ability to do without it. There must be very two before there can be very one. Let it be an alliance of two large formidable natures, mutually beheld, mutually feared, before they yet recognize the deep identity which beneath these disparities unites them.

THE HIGHER THE STYLE we demand of friendship, of course the less easy to establish it with flesh and blood. We walk alone in the world. Friends such as we desire are dreams and fables. But a sublime hope cheers ever the faithful heart, that elsewhere, in other regions of the universal power, souls are now acting, enduring, and daring, which can love us, and which we can love. We may congratulate ourselves that the period of nonage, of follies, of blunders, and of shame, is passed in solitude, and when we are finished men, we shall grasp heroic hands in heroic hands. Only be admonished by what you already see, not to strike leagues of friendship with cheap persons, where no friendship can be. Our impatience betrays us into rash and foolish alliances, which no God attends. By persisting in your path, though you forfeit the little, you gain the great. You become pronounced. You demonstrate yourself, so as to put yourself out of the reach of false relations, and you draw to you the first-born of the world—those rare pilgrims whereof only one or two wander in nature at once, and before whom the vulgar great show as specters and shadows merely.

IT HAS SEEMED TO ME lately more possible than I knew to carry a friendship greatly, on one side, without due correspondence on the other. Why should I cumber myself with regrets that the receiver is not capacious? It never troubles the sun that some of his rays fall wide and vain into ungrateful space, and only a small part on the reflecting planet. Let your greatness educate the crude and cold companion. If he is unequal, he will presently pass away; but thou art enlarged by thy own shining.

Prudence

WHAT RIGHT HAVE I to write on Prudence, whereof I have little, and that of the negative sort? Yet I love facts, and hate lubricity and people without perception. Then I have the same title to write on prudence, that I have to write on poetry or holiness. We write from aspiration and antagonism, as well as from experience. We paint those qualities which we do not possess. The poet admires the man of energy and tactics; the merchant breeds his son for the church or the bar: and where a man is not vain and egotistic, you shall find what he has not by his praise.

Prudence

PRUDENCE IS the virtue of the senses. It is the science of appearances. It is the outmost action of the inward life. It is God taking thought for oxen. It moves matter after the laws of matter. It is content to seek health of body by complying with physical conditions, and health of mind by the laws of the intellect.

The world of the senses is a world of shows; it does not exist for itself, but has a symbolic character; and a true prudence or law of shows recognizes the co-presence of other laws, and knows that its own office is subaltern, knows that it is surface and not center where it works. Prudence is false when detached. It is legitimate when it is the Natural History of the soul incarnate; when it unfolds the beauty of laws within the narrow scope of the senses.

There are all degrees of proficiency in knowledge of the world. It is sufficient to our present purpose to indicate three. One class live to the utility of the symbol; esteeming health and wealth a final good. Another class live above this mark, to the beauty of the symbol; as the poet and artist, and the naturalist, and man of science. A third class live above the beauty of the symbol, to the beauty of the thing signified; these are wise men. The first class have common sense; the second, taste; and the third, spiritual perception.

PRUDENCE DOES NOT GO behind nature, and ask whence it is? It takes the laws of the world, whereby man's being is conditioned, as they are, and keeps these laws, that it may enjoy their proper good. It respects space and time, climate, want, sleep, the law of polarity, growth, and death.

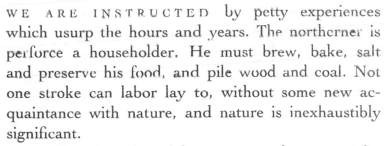

WE ARE INSTRUCTED by petty experiences which usurp the hours and years. The northerner is perforce a householder. He must brew, bake, salt and preserve his food, and pile wood and coal. Not one stroke can labor lay to, without some new acquaintance with nature, and nature is inexhaustibly significant.

Such is the value of these matters, that a man who knows other things, can never know too much of these. Let him have accurate perceptions. Let him, if he have hands, handle; if eyes, measure and discriminate; let him accept and hive every fact of chemistry, natural history, and economics; the more he has, the less is he willing to spare any one. Time is always bringing the occasions that disclose their value. Some wisdom comes out of every natural and innocent action.

The domestic man, who loves no music so well as his kitchen clock, and the airs which the logs sing to him as they burn on the hearth, has solaces which others never dream of. The application of means to ends ensures victory and the songs of victory not less in a farm or a shop than in the tactics of party or of war. The good husband finds method as efficient in the packing of fire-wood in a shed, or in the harvesting of fruits in the cellar, as in Peninsular campaigns or the files of the Department of State. In the rainy day he builds a work-bench, or gets his tool-box set in the corner of the barn-chamber, and stored with nails, gimlet, pincers, screwdriver, and chisel. Herein he tastes an old joy of youth and childhood, the cat-like love of garrets, presses, and corn-chambers, and of the conveniences of long housekeeping. His garden or his poultry-yard—very paltry places, it may be—tell him many pleasant anecdotes. One might find argument for optimism in the abundant flow of this saccharine element of pleasure in every suburb and extremity of the good world. Let a man keep the law—any law—and his way will be strewn with satisfactions. There is more difference in the quality of our pleasures than in the amount.

On the other hand, nature punishes any neglect of prudence. If you think the senses final, obey their law. If you believe in the soul, do not clutch at sensual sweetness before it is ripe on the slow tree of cause and effect. It is vinegar to the eyes, to deal with men of loose and imperfect perception. Dr. Johnson is reported to have said, "If the child says he looked out of this window, when he looked out of that—whip him." Our American character is marked by a more than average delight in accurate perception, which is shown by the currency of the by-word, "No mistake." But the discomfort of unpunctuality, of confusion of thought about facts, of inattention to the wants of tomorrow, is of no nation. The beautiful laws of time and space once dislocated by our inaptitude, are holes and dens. If the hive be disturbed by rash and stupid hands, instead of honey it will yield us bees. Our words and actions to be fair must be timely.

LET HIM PRACTICE the minor virtues. How much of human life is lost in waiting! Let him not make his fellow-creatures wait. How many words and promises are promises of conversation! Let his be words of fate. When he sees a folded and sealed scrap of paper float round the world in a pine ship, and come safe to the eye for which it was written, amidst a swarming population, let him likewise feel the admonition to integrate his being across all these distracting forces, and keep a slender human word among the storms, distances, and accidents that drive us hither and thither, and, by persistency, make the paltry force of one man reappear to redeem its pledge, after months and years, in the most distant climates.

BUT WHAT MAN SHALL DARE tax another with imprudence? Who is prudent? The men we call greatest are least in this kingdom. There is a certain fatal dislocation in our relation to nature, distorting all our modes of living, and making every law our enemy, which seems at last to have aroused all the wit and virtue in the world to ponder the question of Reform. We must call the highest prudence to counsel, and ask why health and beauty and genius should now be the exception, rather than the rule of human nature? Poetry and prudence should be coincident.

We have violated law upon law, until we stand amidst ruins; and when by chance we espy a coincidence between reason and the phenomena, we are surprised.

WE CALL PARTIAL HALF-LIGHTS, by courtesy, genius; talent which converts itself to money, talent which glitters today, that it may dine and sleep well tomorrow; and society is officered by *men of parts*, as they are properly called, and not by divine men. These use their gifts to refine luxury, not to abolish it. Genius is always ascetic, and piety and love. Appetite shows to the finer souls as a disease, and they find beauty in rites and bounds that resist it.

We have found out fine names to cover our sensuality withal, but no gifts can raise intemperance. The man of talent affects to call his transgressions of the laws of the senses trivial, and to count them nothing considered with his devotion to his art. His art rebukes him. That never taught him lewdness, nor the love of wine, nor the wish to reap where he has not sowed. His art is less for every deduction from his holiness, and less for every defect of common sense. On him who scorned the world, as he said, the scorned world wreaks its revenge.

EVERY VIOLATION OF TRUTH is not only a sort of suicide in the liar, but is a stab at the health of human society. On the most profitable lie the course of events presently lays a destructive tax; whilst frankness invites frankness, puts the parties on a convenient footing, and makes their business a friendship.

SO, IN REGARD TO DISAGREEABLE and formidable things, prudence does not consist in evasion, or in flight, but in courage. He who wishes to walk in the most peaceful parts of life with any serenity must screw himself up to resolution. Let him front the object of his worst apprehension, and his stoutness will commonly make his fear groundless. The Latin proverb says that "in battles the eye is first overcome." Entire self-possession may make a battle very little more dangerous to life than a match at foils or at football.

IN THE OCCURRENCE of unpleasant things among neighbors fear comes readily to heart, and magnifies the consequence of the other party; but it is a bad counsellor. Every man is actually weak, and apparently strong. To himself, he seems weak; to others, formidable.

IT IS A PROVERB, that "courtesy costs nothing"; but calculation might come to value love for its profit. Love is fabled to be blind; but kindness is necessary to perception; love is not a hood, but an eye-water. If you meet a sectary, or a hostile partisan, never recognize the dividing lines; but meet on what common ground remains—if only that the sun shines, and the rain rains for both; the area will widen very fast, and ere you know it the boundary mountains, on which the eye had fastened, have melted into air.

Though your views are in straight antagonism to theirs, assume an identity of sentiment, assume that you are saying precisely that which all think, and in the flow of wit and love roll out your paradoxes in solid column, with not the infirmity of a doubt. So at least shall you get an adequate deliverance. The natural motions of the soul are so much better than the voluntary ones, that you will never do yourself justice in dispute. But assume a consent, and it shall presently be granted, since really, and underneath all their external diversities, all men are of one heart and mind.

Wisdom will never let us stand with any man or men on an unfriendly footing. We refuse sympathy and intimacy with people, as if we waited for some better sympathy and intimacy to come. But whence and when? Tomorrow will be like today. Life wastes itself whilst we are preparing to live.

Every man's imagination hath its friends; and pleasant would life be with such companions. But if you cannot have them on good mutual terms, you cannot have them. If not the Deity, but our ambition, hews and shapes the new relations, their virtue escapes, as strawberries lose their flavor in garden-beds.

Thus truth, frankness, courage, love, humility, and all the virtues, range themselves on the side of prudence, or the art of securing a present well-being.

Heroism

LIFE IS A FESTIVAL only to the wise. Seen from the nook and chimney-side of prudence, it wears a ragged and dangerous front. The violations of the laws of nature by our predecessors and our contemporaries are punished in us also. The disease and deformity around us certify the infraction of natural, intellectual, and moral laws, and often violation on violation to breed such compound misery. A lock-jaw that bends a man's head back to his heels; hydrophobia that makes him bark at his wife and babes; insanity that makes him eat grass; war, plague, cholera, famine—[all] indicate a certain ferocity in nature, which, as it had its inlet by human crime, must have its outlet by human suffering. Unhappily, almost no man exists who has not in his own person become, to some amount, a stockholder in the sin, and so made himself liable to a share in the expiation.

Our culture, therefore, must not omit the arming of the man. Let him hear in season that he is born into the state of war, and that the commonwealth and his own well-being require that he should not go dancing in the weeds of peace; but warned, self-collected, and neither defying nor dreading the thunder, let him take both reputation and life in his hand, and with perfect urbanity dare the gibbet and the mob by the absolute truth of his speech and the rectitude of his behavior.

Towards all this external evil the man within the breast assumes a warlike attitude, and affirms his ability to cope single-handed with the infinite army of enemies. To this military attitude of the soul we give the name of heroism. Its rudest form is the contempt for safety and ease, which makes the attractiveness of war. It is a self-trust which slights the restraints of prudence, in the plenitude of its energy and power to repair the harms it may suffer.

The hero is a mind of such balance that no disturbances can shake his will; but pleasantly, and as it were merrily, he advances to his own music, alike in frightful alarms and in the tipsy mirth of universal dissoluteness. There is something not philosophical in heroism; there is something not holy in it; it seems not to know that other souls are of one texture with it; it hath pride; it is the extreme of individual nature. Nevertheless we must profoundly revere it.

Heroism feels and never reasons, and therefore is always right; and although a different breeding, different religion, and greater intellectual activity would have modified or even reversed the particular action, yet for the hero that thing he does is the highest deed, and is not open to the censure of philosophers or divines. It is the avowal of the unschooled man that he finds a quality in him that is negligent of expense, of health, of life, of danger, of hatred, of reproach, and that he knows that his will is higher and more excellent than all actual and all possible antagonists.

Heroism works in contradiction to the voice of mankind, and in contradiction, for a time, to the voice of the great and good. Heroism is an obedience to a secret impulse of an individual's character. Now to no other man can its wisdom appear as it does to him, for every man must be supposed to see a little farther on his own proper path than any one else. Therefore, just and wise men take umbrage at his act, until after some little time be past; then they see it to be in unison with their acts. All prudent men see that the action is clean contrary to a sensual prosperity; for every heroic act measures itself by its contempt of some external good. But it finds its own success at last, and then the prudent also extol.

Self-trust is the essence of heroism. It is the state of the soul at war; and its ultimate objects are the last defiance of falsehood and wrong, and the power to bear all that can be inflicted by evil agents. It speaks the truth, and it is just. It is generous, hospitable, temperate, scornful of petty calculations, and scornful of being scorned. It persists; it is of an undaunted boldness, and of fortitude not to be wearied out. Its jest is the littleness of common life. That false prudence which dotes on health and wealth is the foil, the butt and merriment of heroism.

THE MAGNANIMOUS know very well that they who give time, or money, or shelter to the stranger — so it be done for love, and not for ostentation — do as it were put God under obligation to them, so perfect are the compensations of the universe. In some way, the time they seem to lose is redeemed, and the pains they seem to take remunerate themselves. These men fan the flame of human love, and raise the standard of civil virtue among mankind. But hospitality must be for service, and not for show, or it pulls down the host.

THE ESSENCE OF GREATNESS is the perception that virtue is enough. Poverty is its ornament. Plenty it does not need, and can very well abide its loss.

Heroism

THE CHARACTERISTIC OF HEROISM is its persistency. All men have wandering impulses, fits and starts of generosity. But when you have chosen your part, abide by it, and do not weakly try to reconcile yourself with the world. The heroic cannot be the common, nor the common the heroic. Yet we have the weakness to expect the sympathy of people in those actions whose excellence is that they outrun sympathy, and appeal to a tardy justice.

If you would serve your brother, because it is fit for you to serve him, do not take back your words when you find that prudent people do not commend you. Adhere to your own act, and congratulate yourself if you have done something strange and extravagant, and broken the monotony of a decorous age. It was a high counsel that I once heard given to a young person, "Always do what you are afraid to do."

THERE IS NO WEAKNESS or exposure for which we cannot find consolation in the thought: this is a part of my constitution, part of my relation and office to my fellow-creature. Has nature covenanted with me that I should never appear to disadvantage, never make a ridiculous figure? Let us be generous of our dignity, as well as of our money.

TO SPEAK THE TRUTH even with some austerity, to live with some rigor of temperance or some extremes of generosity, seems to be an ascetism which common good-nature would appoint to those who are at ease and in plenty, in sign that they feel a brotherhood with the great multitude of suffering men. And not only need we breathe and exercise the soul by assuming the penalties of abstinence, of debt, of solitude, of unpopularity, but it behooves the wise man to look with a bold eye into those rarer dangers which sometimes invade men, and to familiarize himself with disgusting forms of disease, with sounds of execration, and the vision of violent death.

I SEE NOT ANY ROAD of perfect peace which a man can walk, but to take counsel of his own bosom. Let him quit too much association; let him go home much, and establish himself in those courses he approves. The unremitting retention of simple and high sentiments in obscure duties is hardening the character to that temper which will work with honor, if need be, in the tumult or on the scaffold.

Heroism

IN THE GLOOM of our ignorance of what shall be in the hour when we are deaf to the higher voices, who does not envy them who have seen safely to an end their manful endeavor? Who that sees the meanness of our politics, but inly congratulates Washington that he is long already wrapped in his shroud, and forever safe; that he was laid sweet in his grave, the hope of humanity not yet subjugated in him? Who does not sometimes envy the good and brave, who are no more to suffer from the tumults of the natural world, and await with curious complacency the speedy term of his own conversation with finite nature? And yet the love that will be annihilated sooner than *[it would be]* treacherous has already made death impossible, and affirms itself no mortal, but a native of the deeps of absolute and inextinguishable being.

Circles

THE EYE IS THE FIRST CIRCLE; the horizon
which it forms is the second; and throughout nature
this primary figure is repeated without end. It is the
highest emblem in the cipher of the world. St. Augustine described the nature of God as a circle whose
center was everywhere, and its circumference nowhere. We are all our lifetime reading the copious
sense of this first of forms. One moral we have already
deduced in considering the circular or compensatory
character of every human action. Another analogy we
shall now trace—that every action admits of being out-
done. Our life is an apprenticeship to the truth that
around every circle another can be drawn; that there is
no end in nature, but every end is a beginning; that
there is always another dawn risen on mid-noon, and
under every deep a lower deep opens.

Circles

There are no fixtures in nature. The universe is fluid and volatile. Permanence is but a word of degrees. Our globe seen by God is a transparent law, not a mass of facts. The law dissolves the fact and holds it fluid. Our culture is the predominance of an idea which draws after it all this train of cities and institutions. Let us rise into another idea, they will disappear.

You admire this tower of granite, weathering the hurts of so many ages. Yet a little waving hand built this huge wall, and that which builds is better than that which is built. The hand that built can topple it down much faster. Better than the hand, and nimbler, was the invisible thought which wrought through it; and thus ever behind the coarse effect is a fine cause, which, being narrowly seen, is itself the effect of a finer cause. Every thing looks permanent until its secret is known.

THE KEY TO EVERY MAN is his thought. Sturdy and defying though he look, he has a helm which he obeys, which is the idea after which all his facts are classified. He can only be reformed by showing him a new idea which commands his own. The life of a man is a self-evolving circle, which, from a ring imperceptibly small, rushes on all sides outward to new and larger circles, and that without end. The extent to which this generation of circles, wheel without wheel, will go, depends on the force or truth of the individual soul. For it is the inert effort of each thought, having formed itself into a circular wave of circumstance — as, for instance, an empire, rules of an art, a local usage, a religious rite — to heap itself on that ridge, and to solidify, and hem in the life. But if the soul is quick and strong, it bursts over that boundary on all sides, and expands another orbit on the great deep, which also runs up into a high wave, with attempt again to stop and to bind. But the heart refuses to be imprisoned; in its first and narrowest pulses it already tends outward with a vast force, and to immense and innumerable expansions.

Every ultimate fact is only the first of a new series. Every general law only a particular fact of some more general law presently to disclose itself. There is no outside, no enclosing wall, no circumference to us.

Fear not the new generalization. Does the fact look crass and material, threatening to degrade thy theory of spirit? Resist it not; it goes to refine and raise thy theory of matter just as much.

OUR MOODS DO NOT BELIEVE in each other. Today I am full of thoughts and can write what I please. I see no reason why I should not have the same thought, the same power of expression, tomorrow. What I write, whilst I write it, seems the most natural thing in the world; but yesterday I saw a dreary vacuity in this direction in which now I see so much; and a month hence, I doubt not, I shall wonder who he was that wrote so many continuous pages. Alas for this infirm faith, this will not strenuous, this vast ebb of a vast flow! I am God in nature; I am a weed by the wall.

EACH NEW STEP we take in thought reconciles twenty seemingly discordant facts, as expressions of one law. Aristotle and Plato are reckoned the respective heads of two schools. A wise man will see that Aristotle platonizes. By going one step further back in thought, discordant opinions are reconciled, by being seen to be extremes of one principle, and we can never go so far back as to preclude a still higher vision.

Beware when the great God lets loose a thinker on this planet. Then all things are at risk. It is as when a conflagration has broken out in a great city, and no man knows what is safe, or where it will end. There is not a piece of science but its flank may be turned tomorrow; there is not any literary reputation, not the so-called eternal names of fame, that may not be revised and condemned. The very hopes of man, the

thoughts of his heart, the religion of nations, the manners and morals of mankind, are all at the mercy of a
new generalization. Generalization is always a new influx of the divinity into the mind. Hence the thrill that
attends it.

Valor consists in the power of self-recovery, so
that a man cannot have his flank turned, cannot be
out-generalled, but put him where you will, he stands.
This can only be by his preferring truth to his past
apprehension of truth, and his alert acceptance of it
from whatever quarter.

There are degrees in idealism. We learn first to
play with it academically, as the magnet was once a
toy. Then we see in the heyday of youth and poetry
that it may be true, that it is true in gleams and frag-
ments. Then its countenance waxes stern and grand,
and we see that it must be true. It now shows itself
ethical and practical. We learn that God IS; that he is
in me; and that all things are shadows of him. The
idealism of Berkeley is only a crude statement of the
idealism of Jesus, and that again is a crude statement
of the fact that all nature is the rapid efflux of goodness executing and organizing itself. Much more obviously is history and the state of the world at any one
time directly dependent on the intellectual classifi-
cation then existing in the minds of men. The things
which are dear to men at this hour are so on account
of the ideas which have emerged on their mental
horizon, and which cause the present order of things,
as a tree bears its apples. A new degree of culture

would instantly revolutionize the entire system of human pursuits.

GOOD AS IS DISCOURSE, silence is better, and shames it. The length of the discourse indicates the distance of thought between the speaker and the hearer. If they were at a perfect understanding in any part, no words would be necessary thereon. If at one in all parts, no words would be suffered.

LITERATURE IS A POINT OUTSIDE of our hodiernal *[i.e., daily]* circle, through which a new one may be described. The use of literature is to afford us a platform whence we may command a view of our present life, a purchase by which we may move it. We fill ourselves with ancient learning, install ourselves the best we can in Greek, in Punic, in Roman houses, only that we may wiselier see French, English, and American houses and modes of living. In like manner, we see literature best from the midst of wild nature, or from the din of affairs, or from a high religion. The field cannot be well seen from within the field. The astronomer must have his diameter of the earth's orbit as a base to find the parallax of any star.

Therefore we value the poet. All the argument and all the wisdom is not in the encyclopedia, or the treatise on metaphysics, or the Body of Divinity, but in the sonnet or the play. In my daily work I incline to repeat my old steps, and do not believe in remedial force, in the power of change and reform. But some Petrarch or Ariosto, filled with the new wine of his imagination, writes me an ode or a brisk romance, full of daring thought and action. He smites and arouses me with his shrill tones, breaks up my whole chain of habits, and I open my eye on my own possibilities. He claps wings to the sides of all the solid old lumber of the world, and I am capable once more of choosing a straight path in theory and practice.

We have the same need to command a view of the religion of the world. We can never see Christianity from the catechism—from the pastures, from a boat in the pond, from amidst the songs of wood-birds, we possibly may. Cleansed by the elemental light and wind, steeped in the sea of beautiful forms which the field offers to us, we may chance to cast a right glance back upon biography *[i.e., upon the life of Jesus]*. Let the claims and virtues of persons be ever so great and welcome, the instinct of man *[nevertheless]* presses eagerly onward to the impersonal and illimitable.

THE NATURAL WORLD may be conceived of as a system of concentric circles, and we now and then detect in nature slight dislocations, which apprize us that this surface on which we now stand is not fixed, but sliding. These manifold tenacious qualities, this chemistry and vegetation, these metals and animals, which seem to stand there for their own sake, are means and methods only—are words of God, and as fugitive as other words. Has the naturalist or chemist learned his craft, who has explored the gravity of atoms and the elective affinities, who has not yet discerned the deeper law whereof this is only a partial or approximate statement, namely, that like draws to like; and that the goods which belong to you gravitate to you, and need not be pursued with pains and cost? Yet is that statement approximate also, and not final. Omnipresence is a higher fact. Not through subtle, subterranean channels need friend and fact be drawn to their counterpart, but, rightly considered, these things proceed from the eternal generation of the soul. Cause and effect are two sides of one fact.

The same law of eternal procession ranges all that we call the virtues, and extinguishes each in the light of a better. The great man will not be prudent in the popular sense; all his prudence will be so much deduction from his grandeur. But it behooves each to see, when he sacrifices prudence, to what god he devotes it; if to ease and pleasure, he had better be prudent still; if to a greater trust, he can well spare his mule and panniers who has a winged chariot instead. Geoffrey draws on his boots to go through the woods, that his feet may be safer from the bite of snakes; Aaron never thinks of such a peril. In many years neither is harmed by such an accident. Yet it seems to me that, with every precaution you take against such an evil, you put yourself into the power of the evil. I suppose that the highest prudence is the lowest prudence.

IT IS THE HIGHEST POWER of divine moments that they abolish our contritions also. I accuse myself of sloth and unprofitableness day by day; but when these waves of God flow into me, I no longer reckon lost time. I no longer poorly compute my possible achievements by what remains to me of the month or the year; for these moments confer a sort of omnipresence and omnipotence which asks nothing of duration, but sees that the energy of the mind is commensurate with the work to be done, without time.

IN NATURE EVERY MOMENT IS NEW; the past is always swallowed and forgotten; the coming only is sacred. Nothing is secure but life, transition, the energizing spirit. No love can be bound by oath or covenant to secure it against a higher love. No truth so sublime but it may be trivial tomorrow in the light of new thoughts. People wish to be settled; only as far as they are unsettled is there any hope for them.

Life is a series of surprises. We do not guess today the mood, the pleasure, the power of tomorrow, when we are building up our being. Of lower states — of acts of routine and sense — we can tell somewhat; but the masterpieces of God, the total growths and universal movements of the soul, he hideth; they are incalculable. I can know that truth is divine and helpful; but how it shall help me I can have no guess, for *so to be* is the sole inlet of *so to know*. The new position of the advancing man has all the powers of the old, yet has them all new. It carries in its bosom all the energies of the past, yet is itself an exhalation of the morning. I cast away in this new moment all my once hoarded knowledge, as vacant and vain. Now, for the first time, seem I to know any thing rightly. The simplest words — we do not know what they mean, except when we love and aspire.

The difference between talents and character is adroitness to keep the old and trodden round, and power and courage to make a new road to new and better goals. Character makes an overpowering present; a cheerful, determined hour, which fortifies all the company, by making them see that much is possible and excellent that was not thought of. Character dulls the impression of particular events. When we see the conqueror, we do not think much of any one battle or success. We see that we had exaggerated the difficulty. It was easy to him. The great man is not convulsible or tormentable; events pass over him without much impression. People say sometimes, "See what I have overcome; see how cheerful I am; see how completely I have triumphed over these black events." Not if they still remind me of the black event. True conquest is the causing the calamity to fade and disappear, as an early cloud of insignificant result in a history so large and advancing.

The one thing which we seek with insatiable desire is to forget ourselves, to be surprised out of our propriety, to lose our sempiternal memory, and to do something without knowing how or why; in short, to draw a new circle. Nothing great was ever achieved without enthusiasm. The way of life is wonderful; it is by abandonment.

Intellect

INTELLECT AND INTELLECTION signify, to the common ear, consideration of abstract truth. The considerations of time and place, of you and me, of profit and hurt, tyrannize over most men's minds. Intellect separates the fact considered from *you*, from all local and personal reference, and discerns it as if it existed for its own sake.

He who is immersed in what concerns person or place cannot see the problem of existence. This the intellect always ponders. Nature shows all things formed and bound. The intellect pierces the form, overleaps the wall, detects intrinsic likeness between remote things, and reduces all things into a few principles.

The making a fact the subject of thought raises it. All that mass of mental and moral phenomena which we do not make objects of voluntary thought come within the power of fortune; they constitute the circumstance of daily life; they are subject to change, to fear, and hope. Every man beholds his human condition with a degree of melancholy. As a ship aground is battered by the waves, so man, imprisoned in mortal life, lies open to the mercy of coming events. But a truth, separated by the intellect, is no longer a subject of destiny. We behold it as a god upraised above care and fear. And so any fact in our life, or any record of our fancies or reflections, disentangled from the web of our unconsciousness, becomes an object impersonal and immortal. What is addressed to us for contemplation does not threaten us, but makes us intellectual beings.

WHATEVER ANY MIND DOES OR SAYS is after a law. It has no random act or word. What has my will done to make me what I am? Nothing. I have been floated into this thought, this hour, this connection of events, by secret currents of might and mind, and my ingenuity and wilfulness have not thwarted, have not aided to an appreciable degree.

Our spontaneous action is always the best. You cannot, with your best deliberation and heed, come so close to any question as your spontaneous glance shall bring you, while you rise from your bed, or walk abroad in the morning, after meditating the matter before sleep on the previous night. Our thinking is a pious reception.

Our truth of thought is therefore vitiated as much by too violent direction given by our will, as by too great negligence. We do not determine what we will think. We only open our senses, clear away, as we can, all obstruction from the fact, and suffer the intellect to see.

We have little control over our thoughts. We are the prisoners of ideas. They catch us up for moments into their heaven, and so fully engage us that we take no thought for the morrow, gaze like children, without an effort to make them our own. By and by we fall out of that rapture, bethink us where we have been, what we have seen, and repeat, as truly as we can, what we have beheld. As far as we can recall these ecstasies, we carry away in the ineffaceable memory the result, and all men and all the ages confirm it. It is called Truth. But the moment we cease to report, and attempt to correct and contrive, it is not truth.

WHAT IS THE HARDEST TASK in the world? To think. I would put myself in the attitude to look in the eye an abstract truth, and I cannot. I blench and withdraw on this side and on that. I seem to know what he meant who said, No man can see God face to face and live. For example, a man explores the basis of civil government. Let him intend his mind without respite, without rest, in one direction. His best heed long time avails him nothing. *[i.e., His best efforts long seem to be in vain.]* Yet thoughts are flitting before him. We all but apprehend, we dimly forebode the truth. We say, I will walk abroad, and the truth will take form and clearness to me. We go forth, but cannot find it. It seems as if we needed only the stillness and composed attitude of the library to seize the thought. But we come in, and are as far from it as at first. Then, in a moment, and unannounced, the truth appears. A certain wandering light appears, and is the distinction, the principle we wanted. But the oracle comes because we had previously laid siege to the shrine.

It seems as if the law of the intellect resembled the law of nature by which we now inspire, now expire the breath; by which the heart now draws in, then hurls out the blood — the law of undulation. So now you must labor with your brains, and now you must forbear your activity, and see what the great Soul showeth.

EACH TRUTH that a writer acquires is a lantern which he turns full on what facts and thoughts lay already in his mind, and behold, all the mats and rubbish which had littered his garret become precious. Every trivial fact in his private biography becomes an illustration of this new principle, revisits the day, and delights all men by its piquancy and new charm. Men say, Where did he get this? and think there was something divine in his life. But no; they have myriads of facts just as good, would they only get a lamp to ransack their attics withal.

EACH MIND has its own method. A true man never acquires after college rules. What you have aggregated in a natural manner surprises and delights when it is produced. For we cannot oversee each other's secret. And hence the differences between men in natural endowment are insignificant in comparison with their common wealth. Do you think the porter and the cook have no anecdotes, no experiences, no wonders for you? Everybody knows as much as the savant. The walls of rude minds are scrawled all over with facts, with thoughts. They shall one day bring a lantern and read the inscriptions. Every man, in the degree in which he has wit and culture, finds his curiosity inflamed concerning the modes of living and thinking of other men, and especially of those classes whose minds have not been subdued by the drill of school education.

WE ARE ALL WISE. The difference between persons is not in wisdom, but in art. Perhaps if we should meet Shakespeare, we should not be conscious of any steep inferiority; no: but of a great equality—only that he possessed a strange skill of using, of classifying his facts, which we lacked. For, notwithstanding our utter incapacity to produce any thing like *Hamlet* and *Othello*, see the perfect reception this wit, and immense knowledge of life, and liquid eloquence find in us all.

IN THE INTELLECT CONSTRUCTIVE, which we popularly designate by the word Genius, we observe the same balance of two elements as in intellect receptive. The constructive intellect produces thoughts, sentences, poems, plans, designs, systems. It is the generation of the mind, the marriage of thought with nature. To genius must always go two gifts, the thought and the publication.

The first is revelation, always a miracle, which no frequency of occurrence or incessant study can ever familiarize, but which must always leave the inquirer stupid with wonder. It is the advent of truth into the world; a form of thought now for the first time bursting into the universe; a child of the old eternal soul; a piece of genuine and immeasurable greatness. It seems, for the time, to inherit all that has yet existed, and to dictate to the unborn. It affects every thought of man, and goes to fashion every institution.

But to make it available, it needs a vehicle or art by which it is conveyed to men. To be communicable, it must become picture or sensible object. We must learn the language of facts. The most wonderful inspirations die with their subject, if he has no hand to paint them to the senses. The ray of light passes invisible through space, and only when it falls on an object is it seen. When the spiritual energy is directed on something outward, then it is a thought. The relation between it and you first makes you, the value of you, apparent to me.

The rich inventive genius of the painter must be smothered and lost for want of the power of drawing; and in our happy hours we should be inexhaustible poets, if once we could break through the silence into adequate rhyme. As all men have some access to primary truth, so all have some art or power of communication in their head; but only in the artist does it descend into the hand. There is an inequality, whose laws we do not yet know, between two men and between two moments of the same man, in respect to this faculty. In common hours we have the same facts as in the uncommon or inspired; but they do not sit for their portraits, they are not detached, but lie in a web.

IT IS TRUE that the discerning intellect of the world is always much in advance of the creative, so that always there are many competent judges of the best book, and few writers of the best books.

THE INTELLECT IS A WHOLE, and demands integrity in every work. This is resisted equally by a man's devotion to a single thought, and by his ambition to combine too many.

Truth is our element of life; yet if a man fasten his attention on a single aspect of truth, and apply himself to that alone for a long time, the truth becomes distorted, and not itself, but falsehood. Herein it resembles the air, which is our natural element, and the breath of our nostrils; but if a stream of the same be directed on the body for a time, it causes cold, fever, and even death.

NEITHER BY DETACHMENT, neither by aggregation, is the integrity of the intellect transmitted to it works, but by a vigilance which brings the intellect in its greatness and best state to operate every moment. It must have the same wholeness which nature has. Although no diligence can rebuild the universe in a model, by the best accumulation or disposition of details, yet does the world reappear in miniature in every event, so that all the laws of nature may be read in the smallest fact. The intellect must have the like perfection in its apprehension and in its works. For this reason, an index or mercury of intellectual proficiency is the perception of identity. We talk with accomplished persons who appear to be strangers in nature. The cloud, the tree, the turf, the bird, are not theirs, have nothing of them; the world is only their lodging and table. But the poet, whose verses are to be spheral and complete, is one whom Nature cannot deceive, whatsoever face of strangeness she may put on. He feels a strict consanguinity, and detects more likeness than variety in all her changes. We are stung by the desire for new thought; but when we receive a new thought, it is only the old thought with a new face; and though we make it our own, we instantly crave another; we are not really enriched. For the truth was in us before it was reflected to us from natural objects; and the profound genius will cast the likeness of all creatures into every product of his wit.

But if the constructive powers are rare, and it is given to few men to be poets, yet every man is a receiver of this descending holy ghost, and may well study the laws of its influx. Exactly parallel is the whole rule of intellectual duty to the rule of moral duty. A self-denial no less austere than the saint's is demanded of the scholar. He must worship truth, and forego all things for that, and choose defeat and pain, so that his treasure in thought is thereby augmented.

THE ANCIENT SENTENCE SAID, Let us be silent, for so are the gods. Silence is a solvent that destroys personality, and gives us leave to be great and universal. Every man's progress is through a succession of teachers, each of whom seems at the time to have a superlative influence, but it at last gives place to a new. Frankly, let him accept it all. Jesus says, Leave father, mother, house and lands, and follow me. Who leaves all receives more. This is as true intellectually as morally. Each new mind we approach seems to require an abdication of all our past and present possessions. A new doctrine seems, at first, a subversion of all our opinions, tastes, and manner of living. Take thankfully and heartily all they can give. Exhaust them, wrestle with them, let them not go until their blessing be won; and after a short season the dismay will be overpast, the excess of influence withdrawn, and they will be no longer an alarming meteor, but one more bright star shining serenely in your heaven, and blending its light with all your day.

But whilst he gives himself up so unreservedly to that which draws him, because that is his own, he is to refuse himself to that which draws him not, whatsoever fame and authority may attend it, because it is not his own. Aeschylus has not yet done his office when he has educated the learned of Europe for a thousand years; he is now to prove himself a master of delight to me also. If he cannot do that, all his fame shall avail him nothing with me.

GOD OFFERS TO EVERY MIND its choice between truth and repose. Take which you please—you can never have both. Between these, as a pendulum, man oscillates ever. He in whom the love of repose predominates will accept the first creed, the first philosophy, the first political party he meets—most likely his father's. He gets rest, commodity, and reputation; but he shuts the door of truth. He in whom the love of truth predominates will keep himself aloof from all moorings and afloat. He will abstain from dogmatism, and recognize all the opposite negations between which, as walls, his being is swung. He submits to the inconvenience of suspense and imperfect opinion; but he is a candidate for truth, as the other is not, and respects the highest law of his being.

Experience

WHERE DO WE FIND OURSELVES? In a series of which we do not know the extremes, and believe that it has none. We wake, and find ourselves on a stair; there are stairs below us, which we seem to have ascended; there are stairs above us, many a one, which go upward and out of sight. But the Genius which, according to the old belief, stands at the door by which we enter, and gives us the lethe to drink, that we may tell no tales, mixed the cup too strongly, and we cannot shake off the lethargy now at noonday. Sleep lingers all our lifetime about our eyes, as night hovers all day in the boughs of the fir-tree. All things swim and glimmer. Our life is not so much threatened as our perception. Ghost-like we glide through nature, and should not know our place again.

Did our birth fall in some fit of indigence and frugality in nature, that she was so sparing of her fire and so liberal of her earth, that it appears to us that we lack the affirmative principle, and though we have health and reason, yet we have no superfluity of spirit for new creation? We have enough to live and bring the year about, but not an ounce to impart or to invest. Ah, that our Genius were a little more of a genius! We are like millers on the lower levels of a stream, when the factories above them have exhausted the water. We, too, fancy that the upper people must have raised their dams.

IN TIMES, when we thought ourselves indolent, we have afterwards discovered that much was accomplished, and much was begun in us. All our days are so unprofitable while they pass, that it is wonderful where or when we ever got anything of this which we call wisdom, poetry, virtue. We never got it on any dated calendar day. Some heavenly days must have been intercalated somewhere, like those that Hermes won with dice of the Moon, that Osiris might be born.

So much of our time is preparation, so much is routine, and so much retrospect, that the pith of each man's genius contracts itself to a very few hours.

PEOPLE GRIEVE and bemoan themselves, but it is not half so bad with them as they say. There are moods in which we court suffering, in the hope that here, at least, we shall find reality, sharp peaks and edges of truth.

I TAKE THIS EVANESCENCE and lubricity of all objects, which lets them slip through our fingers then when we clutch hardest, to be the most unhandsome part of our condition.

DREAM DELIVERS US TO DREAM, and there is no end to illusion. Life is a train of moods like a string of beads, and, as we pass through them, they prove to be many-colored lenses which paint the world their own hue, and each shows only what lies in its focus.

DO YOU SEE THAT KITTEN chasing so prettily her own tail? If you could look with her eyes, you might

see her surrounded with hundreds of figures perform-
ing complex dramas, with tragic and comic issues, long
conversations, many characters, many ups and downs
of fate—and meantime it is only puss and her tail.

OF WHAT USE is fortune or talent to a cold and
defective nature? Of what use is genius, if the organ is
too convex or too concave, and cannot find a focal
distance within the actual horizon of human life?

THE DEFINITION OF *SPIRITUAL* should be,
that which is its own evidence.

HEED THY PRIVATE DREAM: thou wilt not be
missed in the scorning and skepticism: there are
enough of them: stay there in thy closet, and toil, until
the rest are agreed what to do about it. Thy sickness,
they say, and thy puny habit, require that thou do this

or avoid that, but know that thy life is a flitting state, a tent for the night, and do thou, sick or well, finish that stint. Thou art sick, but shalt not be worse, and the universe, which holds thee dear, shall be the better.

E V E R Y   M A N is an impossibility, until he is born; everything impossible, until we see a success. The ardors of piety agree at last with the coldest skepticism — that nothing is of us or our works — that all is of God. Nature will not spare us the smallest leaf of laurel. All writing comes by the grace of God, and all doing and having. I would gladly be moral, and keep due metes and bounds, which I dearly love, and allow the most to the will of man, but I have set my heart on honesty in this chapter, and I can see nothing at last, in success or failure, than more or less of vital force supplied from the Eternal. The results of life are uncalculated and uncalculable. The years teach much which the days never know. The persons who compose our company converse, and come and go, and design and execute many things, and something comes of it all, but an unlooked-for result. The individual is always mistaken. He designed many things, and drew in other persons as coadjutors, quarrelled with some or all, blundered much, and something is done; all are a little advanced, but the individual is always mistaken. It turns out something new, and very unlike what he promised himself.

I AM THANKFUL FOR SMALL MERCIES. I compared notes with one of my friends who expects everything of the universe, and is disappointed when anything is less than the best, and I found that I begin at the other extreme, expecting nothing, and am always full of thanks for moderate goods. I accept the clangor and jangle of contrary tendencies. I find my account in sots and bores also. They give a reality to the circumjacent picture, which such a vanishing meteorous appearance can ill spare. In the morning I awake, and find the old world, wife, babes, and mother, Concord and Boston, the dear old spiritual world, and even the dear old devil not far off. If we will take the good we find, asking no questions, we shall have heaping measures. The great gifts are not got by analysis. Everything good is on the highway. The middle region of our being is the temperate zone. We may climb into the thin and cold realm of pure geometry and lifeless science, or sink into that of sensation. Between these extremes is the equator of life, of thought, of spirit, of poetry—a narrow belt. Moreover, in popular experience, everything good is on the highway.

TO FINISH THE MOMENT, to find the journey's end in every step of the road, to live the greatest number of good hours, is wisdom.

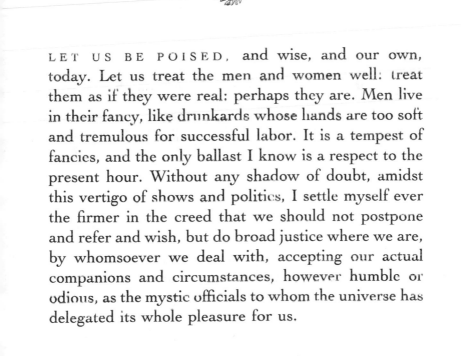

LET US BE POISED, and wise, and our own, today. Let us treat the men and women well: treat them as if they were real: perhaps they are. Men live in their fancy, like drunkards whose hands are too soft and tremulous for successful labor. It is a tempest of fancies, and the only ballast I know is a respect to the present hour. Without any shadow of doubt, amidst this vertigo of shows and politics, I settle myself ever the firmer in the creed that we should not postpone and refer and wish, but do broad justice where we are, by whomsoever we deal with, accepting our actual companions and circumstances, however humble or odious, as the mystic officials to whom the universe has delegated its whole pleasure for us.

Character

THE FACE WHICH CHARACTER wears to me is self-sufficingness. I revere the person who is riches; so that I cannot think of him as alone, or poor, or exiled, or unhappy, or a client, but as perpetual patron, benefactor, and beatified man. Character is centrality, the impossibility of being displaced or overset.

A man should give us a sense of mass. Society is frivolous, and shreds its day into scraps, its conversation into ceremonies and escapes. But if I go to see an ingenious man, I shall think myself poorly entertained if he give me nimble pieces of benevolence and etiquette; rather he shall stand stoutly in his place and let me apprehend, if it were only his resistance, and know that I have encountered a new and positive quality — great refreshment for both of us. It is much that he does not accept the conventional opinions and practices. His nonconformity will remain a goad and a remembrancer, and every inquirer will have to dispose of him, in the first place. *[i.e., Every inquirer will have to begin by coming to terms with him.]*

There is nothing real or useful that is not a seat of war. Our houses ring with laughter and personal and critical gossip, but it helps little. The uncivil, unavailable man, who is a problem and a threat to society, whom it cannot let pass in silence, but must either worship or hate—and to whom all parties feel related, both the leaders of opinion, and the obscure and eccentric—he helps; he puts America and Europe in the wrong, and destroys the skepticism which says, "man is a doll, let us eat and drink, 'tis the best we can do," by illuminating the untried and unknown.

Acquiescence in the establishment, and appeal to the public, indicate infirm faith, heads which are not clear, and which must see a house built before they can comprehend the plan of it.

CHARACTER IS A NATURAL POWER, like light and heat, and all nature cooperates with it. The reason why we feel one man's presence, and do not feel another's, is as simple as gravity. Truth is the summit of being: justice is the application of it to affairs. All individual natures stand in a scale, according to the purity of this element in them. The will of the pure runs down from them into other natures, as water runs down from a higher into a lower vessel. This natural force is no more to be withstood than any other natural force. We can drive a stone upward for a moment into the air, but it is yet true that all stones will for ever fall; and whatever instances can be quoted of unpunished theft, or of a lie which somebody credited, justice must prevail, and it is the privilege of truth to make itself believed. Character is this moral order seen through the medium of an individual nature. Men of character are the conscience of the society to which they belong.

WE HAVE NO PLEASURE in thinking of a benevolence that is only measured by its works. Love is inexhaustible, and if its estate is wasted, its granary emptied, still cheers and enriches, and the man, though he sleep, seems to purify the air, and his house to adorn the landscape and strengthen the laws. People always recognize this difference. We know who is benevolent, by quite other means than the amount of subscription to soup-societies. It is only low merits that can be enumerated.

The longest list of specifications of benefit would look very short. A man is a poor creature if he is to be measured so. The rule and hodiernal *[i.e., ∂aily]* life of a good man is benefaction.

I KNOW NOTHING which life has to offer so satisfying as the profound good understanding which can subsist, after much exchange of good offices, between two virtuous men, each of whom is sure of himself and sure of his friend. It is a happiness which postpones all other gratifications and makes politics, and commerce, and churches, cheap. For, when men shall meet as they ought, each a benefactor, a shower of stars, clothed with thoughts, with deeds, with accomplishments, it should be the festival of nature which all things announce. A divine person is the prophecy of the mind; a friend is the hope of the heart. Our beatitude waits for the fulfilment of these two in one.

Gifts

FOR COMMON GIFTS, necessity makes perti-
nences and beauty every day, and one is glad when an
imperative leaves him no option, since if the man at the
door has no shoes you have not to consider whether
you could procure him a paint-box. And as it is always
pleasing to see a man eat bread, or drink water, in the
house or out of doors, so it is always a great satisfaction to supply these first wants. Necessity does everything well. In our condition of universal dependence, it
seems heroic to let the petitioner be the judge of his
necessity, and to give all that is asked, though at great
inconvenience. If it be a fantastic desire, it is better to
leave to others the office of punishing him. I can think
of many parts I should prefer playing to that of the
Furies.

OUR TOKENS of compliment and love are for the most part barbarous. Rings and other jewels are not gifts, but apologies for gifts. The only gift is a portion of thyself. Thou must bleed for me. Therefore the poet brings his poem; the shepherd, his lamb; the farmer, corn; the miner, a gem; the sailor, coral and shells; the painter, his picture; the girl, a handkerchief of her own sewing. This is right and pleasing, for it restores society in so far to its primary basis, when a man's biography is conveyed in his gift, and every man's wealth is an index of his merit. But it is a cold, lifeless business when you go to the shops to buy me something, which does not represent your life and talent, but a goldsmith's.

WE ASK THE WHOLE. Nothing less will content us. We arraign society if it do not give us, besides earth, and fire, and water, opportunity, love, reverence, and objects of veneration.

WE WISH TO BE SELF-SUSTAINED. We do not quite forgive a giver. The hand that feeds us is

in some danger of being bitten. We can receive anything from love, for that is a way of receiving it from
ourselves; but not from anyone who assumes to bestow.

He is a good man who can receive a gift well. We
are either glad or sorry at a gift, and both emotions are
unbecoming. Some violence, I think, is done, some
degradation borne, when I rejoice or grieve at a gift. I
am sorry when my independence is invaded, or when
a gift comes from such as do not know my spirit, and
so the act is not supported; and if the gift pleases me
overmuch, then I should be ashamed that the donor
should read my heart, and see that I love his commodity, and not him.

THE EXPECTATION of gratitude is mean, and is
continually punished by the total insensibility of the
obliged person. It is a great happiness to get off without
injury and heart-burning from one who has had the ill-
luck to be served by you. It is a very onerous business,
this of being served, and the debtor naturally wishes to
give you a slap. A golden text for these gentlemen is that
which I so admire in the Buddhist, who never thanks,
and who says, "Do not flatter your benefactors."

COMPARED WITH that good-will I bear my friend, the benefit it is in my power to render him seems small.

THE BEST of hospitality and of generosity is not in the will, but in fate. I find that I am not much to you; you do not need me; you do not feel me; then I am thrust out of doors, though you proffer me house and land. No services are of any value, but only likeness. When I have attempted to join myself to others by services, it proved an intellectual trick—no more. They eat your service like apples, and leave you out. But love them, and they feel you, and delight in you all the time.

Nature

THERE ARE DAYS which occur in this climate, at almost any season of the year, wherein the world reaches its perfection, when the air, the heavenly bodies, and the earth make a harmony, as if nature would indulge her offspring; when, in these bleak upper sides of the planet, nothing is to desire that we have heard of the happiest latitudes, and we bask in the shining hours of Florida and Cuba; when everything that has life gives sign of satisfaction, and the cattle that lie on the ground seem to have great and tranquil thoughts. These halcyons may be looked for with a little more assurance in that pure October weather which we distinguish by the name of the Indian Summer. The day, immeasurably long, sleeps over the broad hills and warm wide fields. To have lived through all its sunny hours seems longevity enough.

AT THE GATES OF THE FOREST, the surprised man of the world is forced to leave his city estimates of great and small, wise and foolish. The knapsack of custom falls off his back with the first step he makes into these precincts. Here is sanctity which shames our religions, and reality which discredits our heroes. Here we find nature to be the circumstance which dwarfs every other circumstance, and judges like a god all men that come to her.

We have crept out of our close and crowded houses into the night and morning, and we see what majestic beauties daily wrap us in their bosom. How willingly we would escape the barriers which render them comparatively impotent, escape the sophistication and second thought, and suffer nature to intrance us.

The tempered light of the woods is like a perpetual morning, and is stimulating and heroic. The anciently reported spells of these places creep on us. The stems of pines, hemlocks, and oaks almost gleam like iron on the excited eye. The incommunicable trees begin to persuade us to live with them, and quit our life of solemn trifles. Here no history, or church, or state, is interpolated on the divine sky and the immortal year. How easily we might walk onward into the opening landscape, absorbed by new pictures, and by thoughts fast succeeding each other, until by degrees the recollection of home was crowded out of the mind, all memory obliterated by the tyranny of the present, and we were led in triumph by nature.

These enchantments are medicinal; they sober and heal us. These are plain treasures, kindly and native to us. We come to our own and make friends with matter, which the ambitious chatter of the schools would persuade us to despise. We never can part with it; the mind loves its old home: as water to our thirst, so is the rock, the ground, to our eyes, and hands, and feet.

CITIES GIVE NOT the human senses room enough. We go out daily and nightly to feed the eyes on the horizon, and require so much scope, just as we need water for our bath.

IT SEEMS AS IF the day was not wholly profane, in which we have given heed to some natural object.

My house stands on low land, with limited outlook, and on the skirt of the village. But I go with my friend to the shore of our little river, and with one stroke of the paddle, I leave the village politics and

personalities, yes, and the world of villages and personalities, behind, and pass into a delicate realm of
sunset and moonlight, too bright almost for spotted
man to enter without noviciate and probation.

We penetrate bodily this incredible beauty; we
dip our hands into this painted element; our eyes
are bathed in these lights and forms. A holiday, a
royal revel, the proudest, most heart-rejoicing festival
that valor and beauty, power and taste, ever decked
and enjoyed, establishes itself on the instant. These
sunset clouds, these delicately emerging stars, with
their private and ineffable glances, signify it and
proffer it.

I am taught the poorness of our invention, the
ugliness of towns and palaces. Art and luxury have
early learned that they must work as enhancement
and sequel to this original beauty. I am over-
instructed for my return. Henceforth I shall be hard
to please. I cannot go back to toys. I am grown
expensive and sophisticated. I can no longer live
without elegance; but a countryman shall be my master of revels. He who knows the most, he who knows
what sweets and virtues are in the ground, the waters, the plants, the heavens, and how to come at
these enchantments, is the rich and royal man. Only
as far as the masters of the world have called in nature to their aid can they reach the height of mag-
nificence. This is the meaning of their hanging
gardens, villas, garden-houses, islands, parks, and
preserves, to back their faulty personality with these
strong accessories.

Nature

LITERATURE, POETRY, SCIENCE, are the homage of man to this unfathomed secret, concerning which no sane man can affect an indifference or incuriosity. Nature is loved by what is best in us. It is loved as the city of God, although, or rather because there is no citizen. The sunset is unlike anything that is underneath it: it wants men. And the beauty of nature must always seem unreal and mocking, until the landscape has human figures that are as good as itself. If there were good men, there would never be this rapture in nature.

Man is fallen; nature is erect, and serves as a differential thermometer, detecting the presence or absence of the divine sentiment in man. By fault of our dullness and selfishness, we are looking up to nature, but when we are convalescent, nature will look up to us. We see the foaming brook with compunction: if our own life flowed with the right energy, we should shame the brook. The stream of zeal sparkles with real fire, and not with reflex rays of sun and moon.

MOTION OR CHANGE, and identity or rest, are the first and second secrets of nature: Motion and

Rest. The whole code of her laws may be written on the thumbnail, or the signet of a ring. The whirling bubble on the surface of a brook admits us to the secret of the mechanics of the sky. Every shell on the beach is a key to it. A little water made to rotate in a cup explains the formation of the simpler shells; the addition of matter from year to year arrives at last at the most complex forms; and yet so poor is nature with all her craft, that, from the beginning to the end of the universe, she has but one stuff—but one stuff with two ends, to serve up all her dream-like variety. Compound it how she will, star, sand, fire, water, tree, man, it is still one stuff, and betrays the same properties.

Things are so strictly related that, according to the skill of the eye, from any one object the parts and properties of any other may be predicted. If we had eyes to see it, a bit of stone from the city wall would certify us of the necessity that man must exist as readily as [would] the city. That identity makes us all one, and reduces to nothing great intervals on our customary scale. We talk of deviations from natural life, as if artificial life were not also natural. The smoothest curled courtier in the boudoirs of a palace has an animal nature, rude and aboriginal as a white bear, omnipotent to its own ends, and is directly related there, amid essences and billets-doux, to Himalayan mountain-chains and the axis of the globe.

If we consider how much we are nature's, we need not be superstitious about towns, as if that terrific or benefic force did not find us there also, and fashion cities. Nature, who made the mason, made the house. We may easily hear too much of rural influences. The cool, disengaged air of natural objects makes them enviable to us, chafed and irritable creatures with red faces, and we think we shall be as grand as they, if we camp out and eat roots; but let us be men instead of woodchucks, and the oak and the elm shall gladly serve us, though we sit in chairs of ivory on carpets of silk.

EXAGGERATION IS in the course of things. Nature sends no creature, no man into the world without adding a small excess of his proper quality. Given the planet, it is still necessary to add the impulse; so, to every creature nature added a little violence of direction in its proper path, a shove to put it on its way; in every instance, a slight generosity, a drop too much. Without electricity the air would rot; and without this violence of direction which men and women have, without a spice of bigot and fanatic, no excitement, no efficiency. We aim above the mark, to hit the mark.

The vegetable life does not content itself with casting from the flower or the tree a single seed, but it fills the air and earth with a prodigality of seeds, that, if thousands perish, thousands may plant themselves, that hundreds may come up, that tens may live to maturity, that, at least, one may replace the parent. All things betray the same calculated profusion. The excess of fear with which the animal frame is hedged round—shrinking from cold, starting at the sight of a snake or at a sudden noise—protects us, through a multitude of groundless alarms, from some one real danger at last.

THE CRAFT with which the world is made runs also into the mind and character of men. No man is quite sane; each has a vein of folly in his composition, a slight determination of the blood to the head, to make sure of holding him hard to some one point which nature had taken to heart. Great causes are never tried on their merits; but the cause is reduced to particulars to suit the size of the partisans, and the contention is ever hottest on minor matters. Not less remarkable is the overfaith of each man in the importance of what he has to do or say. The poet, the prophet, has a higher value for what he utters than any hearer, and therefore it gets spoken.

One may have impressive experience, and yet may not know how to put his private fact into literature; and perhaps the discovery that wisdom has other tongues and ministers than we, that though we should hold our peace, the truth would not the less be spoken, might check injuriously the flames of our zeal. A man can only speak, so long as he does not feel his speech to be partial and inadequate. It is partial, but he does not see it to be so while he utters it. As soon as he is released from the instinctive and particular, and sees its partiality, he shuts his mouth in disgust. For no man can write anything who does not think that what he writes is, for the time, the history of the world; or do anything well, who does not esteem his work to be of importance. My work may be of none, but I must not think it of none, or I shall not do it with impunity.

In like manner, there is throughout nature something mocking, something that leads us on and on, but arrives nowhere, keeps no faith with us. All promise outruns the performance. We live in a system of approximations. Every end is prospective of some other end, which is also temporary; a round and final success nowhere. We are encamped in nature, not domesticated. Hunger and thirst lead us on to eat and to drink; but bread and wine, mix and cook them how you will, leave us hungry and thirsty, after the stomach is full. It is the same with all our arts and performances. Our music, our poetry, our language itself are not satisfactions, but suggestions.

The hunger for wealth, which reduces the planet to a garden, fools the eager pursuer. What is the end sought? Plainly to secure the ends of good sense and beauty from the intrusion of deformity or vulgarity of any kind. Conversation, character, were the avowed ends; wealth was good as it appeased the animal cravings, cured the smoky chimney, silenced the creaking door, brought friends together in a warm and quiet room, and kept the children and the dinner-table in a different apartment *[i.e., room]*. Thought, virtue, beauty, were the ends; but it was known that men of thought and virtue sometimes had the headache, or wet feet, or could lose good time while the room was getting warm in winter days. Unluckily, in the exertions necessary to remove these inconveniences the main attention has been diverted to this object; the old aims have been lost sight of, and to remove friction has come to be the end. That is the ridicule of rich men — that they arrive with pains and sweat and fury nowhere; when all is done, it is for nothing. They are like one who has interrupted the conversation of a company to make his speech, and now has forgotten what he went to say. The appearance strikes the eye everywhere of an aimless society, of aimless nations. Boston, London, Vienna, and now the governments generally of the world, are cities and governments of the rich, and the masses are not men, but *poor men,* that is, men who would be rich. Were the ends of nature so great and cogent as to exact this immense sacrifice of men?

TO THE INTELLIGENT, nature converts itself into a vast promise, and will not be rashly explained. Her secret is untold. Many and many an Oedipus arrives: he has the whole mystery teeming in his brain. Alas! the same sorcery has spoiled his skill; no syllable can he shape on his lips. Her mighty orbit vaults like the fresh rainbow into the deep, but no archangel's wing was yet strong enough to follow it and report upon the return of the curve. But it also appears that our actions are seconded and disposed to greater conclusions than we designed. We are escorted on every hand through life by spiritual agents, and a beneficent purpose lies in wait for us. We cannot bandy words with nature, or deal with her as we deal with persons. If we measure our individual forces against hers, we may easily feel as if we were the sport of an insuperable destiny. But if, instead of identifying ourselves with the work, we feel that the soul of the workman streams through us, we shall find the peace of the morning dwelling first in our hearts, and the fathomless powers of gravity and chemistry, and, over them, of life, pre-existing within us in their highest form.

The uneasiness which the thought of our helplessness in the chain of causes occasions us, results from looking too much at one condition of nature, namely, Motion. But the drag is never taken from the wheel. Wherever the impulse exceeds, the Rest or Identity insinuates its compensation. All over the wild fields of earth grows the prunella or self-heal. After every foolish day we sleep off the fumes and furies of its hours; and though we are always engaged with particulars, and often enslaved to them, we bring with us to every experiment the innate universal laws. These, while they exist in the mind as ideas, stand around us in nature for ever embodied, a present sanity to expose and cure the insanity of men.

LET THE VICTORY FALL where it will, we are on that side. And the knowledge that we traverse the whole scale of being, from the center to the poles of nature, and have some stake in every possibility, lends that sublime luster to death, which philosophy and religion have too outwardly and literally striven to express in the popular doctrine of the immortality of the soul. The reality is more excellent than the report.

EVERY MOMENT INSTRUCTS, and every object: for wisdom is infused into every form. It has been poured into us as blood; it convulsed us as pain; it slid into us as pleasure; it enveloped us in dull, melancholy days, or in days of cheerful labor; we did not guess its essence, until after a long time.

Politics

IN DEALING WITH THE STATE, we ought to remember that its institutions are not aboriginal, though they existed before we were born: that they are not superior to the citizen: that every one of them was once the act of a single man: every law and usage was a man's expedient to meet a particular case: that they all are imitable, all alterable; we may make as good: we may make better. Society is an illusion to the young citizen. It lies before him in rigid repose, with certain names, men, and institutions, rooted like oak trees to the center, round which all arrange themselves the best they can. But the old statesman knows that society is fluid; there are no such roots and centers; but any particle may suddenly become the center of the movement, and compel the system to gyrate round it, as every man of strong will, like Pisistratus, or Crom-

well, does for a time, and every man of truth, like
Plato, or Paul, does for ever.

THE WISE KNOW that foolish legislation is a rope
of sand, which perishes in the twisting; that the State
must follow, and not lead the character and progress of
the citizen; the strongest usurper is quickly got rid of;
and they only who build on Ideas, build for eternity;
and that the form of government which prevails is the
expression of what cultivation exists in the population
which permits it. The law is only a memorandum. We
are superstitious, and esteem the statute as something
[in itself]: so much life as it has in the character of
living men, is its force.

THE THEORY OF POLITICS which has pos-
sessed the mind of men, and which they have expressed
the best they could in their laws and in their revolutions, considers persons and property as the two objects for whose protection government exists. Of
persons, all have equal rights, in virtue of being identical in nature. This interest, of course, with its whole

power demands a democracy. While the rights of all as persons are equal, in virtue of their access to reason, their rights in property are very unequal. One man owns his clothes, and another owns a county. This accident, depending, primarily, on the skill and virtue of the parties, of which there is every degree, and, secondarily, on patrimony, falls unequally, and its rights, of course, are unequal. Personal rights, universally the same, demand a government framed on the ratio of the census: property demands a government framed on the ratio of owners and of owning.

It was not, however, found easy to embody the readily-admitted principle that property should make law for property, and persons for persons: since persons and property mixed themselves in every transaction. At last it seemed settled, that the rightful distinction was that the proprietors should have more elective franchise than non-proprietors, on the Spartan principle of "calling that which is just, equal; not that which is equal, just."

That principle no longer looks so self-evident as it appeared in former times, partly, because doubts have arisen whether too much weight had not been allowed in the laws to property, and such a structure given to our usages as allowed the rich to encroach on the poor, and to keep them poor; but mainly, because there is an instinctive sense, however obscure and yet inarticulate, that the whole constitution of property, on its present tenures, is injurious, and its influence on persons deteriorating and degrading; that truly, the only interest for the consideration of the State is persons: that property will always follow persons; that the highest end of government is the culture of men: and if men can be educated, the institutions will share their improvement, and the moral sentiment will write the law of the land.

If it be not easy to settle the equity of this question, the peril is less when we take note of our natural defences. We are kept by better guards than the vigilance of such magistrates as we commonly elect. Society always consists, in greatest part, of young and foolish persons. The old, who have seen through the hypocrisy of courts and statesmen, die, and leave no wisdom to their sons. They believe their own newspapers, as their fathers did at their age. With such an ignorant and deceivable majority, States would soon run to ruin, but that there are limitations, beyond which the folly and ambition of governors cannot go. Things have their laws, as well as men; and things refuse to be trifled with. Property will be protected. Corn will not grow unless it is planted and manured; but the farmer will not plant or hoe it unless the chances are a hundred to one that he will cut and harvest it. Under any forms, persons and property must and will have their just sway. They exert their power, as steadily as matter its attraction.

The boundaries of personal influence it is impossible to fix, as persons are organs of moral or supernatural force. Under the dominion of an idea, which possesses the minds of multitudes, as civil freedom, or the religious sentiment, the powers of persons are no longer subjects of calculation. A nation of men unanimously bent on freedom, or conquest, can easily confound the arithmetic of statists and achieve extravagant actions, out of all proportion to their means; as the Greeks, the Saracens, the Swiss, the Americans, and the French have done.

THE SAME NECESSITY which secures the rights of person and property against the malignity or folly of the magistrate, determines the form and methods of governing which are proper to each nation, and to its habit of thought, and nowise transferable to other states of society. In this country, we are very vain of our political institutions, which are singular in this, that they sprung, within the memory of living men, from the character and condition of the people, which they still express with sufficient fidelity — and we ostentatiously prefer them to any other in history. They are not better, but only fitter for us. We may be wise in asserting the advantage in modern times of the democratic form, but to other states of society, in which religion consecrated the monarchical, that, and not this, was expedient. Democracy is better for us, because the religious sentiment of the present time accords better with it. Born democrats, we are nowise qualified to judge of monarchy, which, to our fathers living in the monarchical idea, was also relatively right.

OUR INSTITUTIONS, though in coincidence with the spirit of the age, have not any exemption from the practical defects which have discredited other forms. Every actual State is corrupt. Good men must not obey the laws too well. What satire on government can equal the severity of censure conveyed in the word *politic,* which now for ages has signified cunning, intimating that the State is a trick?

The same benign necessity and the same practical abuse appear in the parties into which each State divides itself, of opponents and defenders of the administration of the government. Parties are also founded on instincts, and have better guides to their own humble aims than the sagacity of their leaders. They have nothing perverse in their origin, but rudely mark some real and lasting relation. We might as wisely reprove the east wind, or the frost, as a political party, whose members, for the most part, could give no account of their position, but stand for the defence of those interests in which they find themselves. Our quarrel with them begins when they quit this deep natural ground at the bidding of some leader, and, obeying personal considerations throw themselves into the maintenance and defence of points nowise belonging to their system.

A party is perpetually corrupted by personality. While we absolve the association from dishonesty, we cannot extend the same charity to their leaders. They reap the rewards of the docility and zeal of the masses, which they direct. Ordinarily, our parties are parties of circumstances, and not of principle; as, the planting interest in conflict with the commercial; the party of capitalists, and that of operatives; parties which are identical in their moral character, and which can easily change ground with each other, in the support of many of their measures. Parties of principle, as, religious sects, or the party of free-trade, of universal suffrage, of abolition of slavery, of abolition of capital punishment, degenerate into personalities, or would inspire enthusiasm. The vice of our leading parties in this country (which may be cited as a fair specimen of these societies of opinion) is, that they do not plant themselves on the deep and necessary grounds to which they are respectively entitled, but lash themselves to fury in the carrying of some local and momentary measure, nowise useful to the commonwealth.

Of the two great parties which, at this hour, almost share the nation between them, I should say that one has the best cause, and the other contains the best men. The philosopher, the poet, or the religious man will, of course, wish to cast his vote with the democrat, for free-trade, for wide suffrage, for the abolition of

legal cruelties in the penal code, and for facilitating in
every manner the access of the young and the poor to
the sources of wealth and power. But he can rarely
accept the persons whom the so-called popular party
propose to him as representatives of these liberalities.
They have not at heart the ends which give to the name
of democracy what hope and virtue are in it. The spirit
of our American radicalism is destructive and aimless:
it is not loving; it has no ulterior and divine ends; but
is destructive only out of hatred and selfishness.

On the other side, the conservative party, composed of the most moderate, able, and cultivated part
of the population, is timid, and merely defensive of
property. It vindicates no right, it aspires to no real
good, it brands no crime, it proposes no generous pol-
icy, it does not build, nor write, nor cherish the arts,
nor foster religion, nor establish schools, nor encour-
age science, nor emancipate the slave, nor befriend the
poor, or the Indian, or the immigrant. From neither
party, when in power, has the world any benefit to
expect in science, art, or humanity, at all commensurate with the resources of the nation.

THE FACT OF TWO POLES, of two forces, cen-
tripetal and centrifugal, is universal, and each force, by
its own activity, develops the other. Wild liberty de-

velops iron conscience. Want of liberty, by strength-
ening law and decorum, stupefies conscience.

WE MUST TRUST INFINITELY to the beneficent necessity which shines through all laws. Human
nature expresses itself in them as characteristically as
in statues, or songs, or railroads, and an abstract of the
codes of nations would be a transcript of the common
conscience. Governments have their origin in the moral
identity of men. Reason for one is seen to be reason for
another, and for every other. There is a middle measure which satisfies all parties, be they never so many,
or so resolute for their own. Every man finds a sanc-
tion for his simplest claims and deeds in decisions of
his own mind, which he calls truth and holiness. In
these decisions all the citizens find a perfect agree-
ment, and only in these: not in what is good to eat,
good to wear, good use of time, or what amount of
land, or of public aid, each is entitled to claim.

This truth and justice men presently endeavor
to make application of, to the measuring of land, the
apportionment of service, the protection of life and
property. Their first endeavors, no doubt, are very
awkward. Yet absolute right is the first governor; or,
every government is an impure theocracy. The idea,
after which each community is aiming to make and
mend its law, is the will of the wise man. The wise

man, it cannot find in nature, and it makes awkward but earnest efforts to secure his government by contrivance.

Every man's nature is a sufficient advertisement to him of the character of his fellows. My right and my wrong, is their right and their wrong. While I do what is fit for me, and abstain from what is unfit, my neighbor and I shall often agree in our means, and work together for a time to one end. But whenever I find my dominion over myself not sufficient to me, and undertake the direction of him also, I overstep the truth, and come into false relations to him. I may have so much more skill or strength than he, that he cannot express adequately his sense of wrong, but it is a lie, and hurts like a lie both him and me. Love and nature cannot maintain the assumption: it must be executed by a practical lie, namely, by force. This undertaking for another is the blunder which stands in colossal ugliness in the governments of the world.

It is the same thing in numbers, as in a pair, only not quite so intelligible. I can see well enough a great difference between my setting myself down to a self-control, and my going to make somebody else act after my views; but when a quarter of the human race assume to tell me what I must do, I may be too much disturbed by the circumstances to see so clearly the absurdity of their command. Therefore, all public ends look vague and quixotic beside private ones. For, any laws but those which men make for themselves are laughable.

If I put myself in the place of my child, and we

stand in one thought, and see what things are thus or
thus, that perception is law for him and me. We are
both there, both act. But if, without carrying him into
the thought, I look over into his plot, and, guessing
how it is with him, ordain this or that, he will never
obey me. This is the history of governments — one man
does something which is to bind another. A man who
cannot be acquainted with me, taxes me; looking from
afar at me, ordains that a part of my labor shall go to
this or that whimsical end, not as I, but as he happens
to fancy. Behold the consequence. Of all debts, men
are least willing to pay the taxes. What a satire is this
on government! Everywhere they think they get their
money's worth, except for these.

Hence, the less government we have, the better —
the fewer laws, and the less confided power. The an-
tidote to this abuse of formal government is the
influence of private character, the growth of the individual; the appearance of the principal to supersede
the proxy; the appearance of the wise man, of whom
the existing government is, it must be owned, a shabby
imitation. That which all things tend to educe, which
freedom, cultivation, intercourse, revolutions, go to
form and deliver, is character: that is the end of nature, to reach unto this coronation of her king. To
educate the wise man, the State exists; and with the
appearance of the wise man, the State expires. The
appearance of character makes the State unnecessary.

The wise man is the State. He needs no army,
fort, or navy — he loves men too well; no bribe, or

feast, or palace, to draw friends to him: no vantage
ground, no favorable circumstance. He needs no library, for he is done thinking; no church, for he is a
prophet; no statute book, for he is the lawgiver; no
money, for he is value; no road, for he is at home
where he is; no experience, for the life of the creator
shoots through him, and looks from his eyes. He has
no personal friends, for he who has the spell to draw
the prayer and piety of all men unto him, needs not
husband and educate a few, to share with him a select
and poetic life. His relation to men is angelic; his memory is myrrh to them; his presence, frankincense and
flowers.

We think our civilization near its meridian, but we
are yet only at the cock-crowing and the morning star.
In our barbarous society the influence of character is
in its infancy. As a political power, as the rightful lord
who is to tumble all rulers from their chairs, its presence is hardly yet suspected.

IT IS BECAUSE WE KNOW how much is due
from us that we are impatient to show some petty
talent as a substitute for worth. We are haunted by a
conscience of this right to grandeur of character, and
are false to it. But each of us has some talent, can do
something useful, or graceful, or formidable, or amus-

ing, or lucrative. That we do, as an apology to others and to ourselves for not reaching the mark of a good and equal life. But it does not satisfy *us*, while we thrust it on the notice of our companions. It may throw dust in their eyes, but does not smooth our own brow, or give us the tranquillity of the strong when we walk abroad. We do penance as we go. Our talent is a sort of expiation, and we are constrained to reflect on our splendid moment, with a certain humiliation, as something too fine, and not as one act of many acts, a fair expression of our permanent energy.

Senators and presidents have climbed so high with pain enough, not because they think the place especially agreeable, but as an apology for real worth, and to vindicate their manhood in our eyes. This conspicuous chair is their compensation to themselves for being of a poor, cold, hard nature.

If a man found himself so rich-natured that he could enter into strict relations with the best persons, and make life serene around him by the dignity and sweetness of his behavior, could he afford circumventions to win favor with the caucus and the press, or engage in covert relations so hollow and pompous as those of a politician? Surely nobody would be a charlatan, who could afford to be sincere.

The tendencies of the times favor the idea of self-government, and leave the individual, for all code, to the rewards and penalties of his own constitution, which work with more energy than we believe, while we depend on artificial restraints. The movement in this direction has been very marked in modern history. Much has been blind and discreditable, but the nature of the revolution is not affected by the vices of the revolters, for this is a purely moral force. It was never adopted by any party in history, neither can be. It separates the individual from all party, and unites him, at the same time, to the race. It promises a recognition of higher rights than those of personal freedom, or the security of property. A man has a right to be employed, to be trusted, to be loved, to be revered.

The power of love, as the basis of a state, has never been tried. We must not imagine that all things are lapsing into confusion, if every tender protester be not compelled to bear his own part in certain social conventions: nor doubt that roads can be built, letters carried, and the fruit of labor secured, when the government of force is at an end. Are our methods now so excellent that all competition is hopeless? Could not a nation of friends even devise better ways? On the other hand, let not the most conservative and timid fear anything from a premature surrender of the bayonet and the system of force. For, according to the order of nature, which is quite superior to our will, it stands thus: there will always be a government of force where men are selfish; and when they are pure enough to abjure the code of force, they will be wise enough to see how these public ends of the post-office, of the highway, of commerce, and the exchange of property, of museums and libraries, of institutions of art and science, can be answered.

Politics

We live in a very low state of the world, and pay unwilling tribute to governments founded on force. There is not, among the most religious and instructed men of the most religious and civil nations, a reliance on the moral sentiment, and a sufficient belief in the unity of things to persuade them that society can be maintained without artificial restraints, as well as the solar system; or that the private citizen might be reasonable, and a good neighbor, without the hint of a jail or a confiscation. What is strange too, there never was in any man sufficient faith in the power of rectitude to inspire him with the broad design of renovating the State on the principle of right and love. All those who have pretended this design have been partial reformers, and have admitted in some manner the supremacy of the bad State. *[But]* I have just been conversing with one man, to whom no weight of adverse experience will make it for a moment appear impossible that thousands of human beings might exercise towards each other the grandest and simplest sentiments, as well as a knot of friends, or a pair of lovers.

The Transcendentalist

Note: "The Transcendentalist" is a lecture that Emerson delivered in Boston in January 1842. Although not published in the first or second series of Essays, *it is included here because it is such an important statement of some of Emerson's key beliefs.*

WHAT IS POPULARLY CALLED Transcendentalism among us, is Idealism; Idealism as it appears in 1842. As thinkers, mankind have ever divided into two sects, Materialists and Idealists; the first class founding on experience, the second on consciousness; the first class beginning to think from the data of the senses, the second class perceive that the senses are not final, and say, the senses give us representations of things, but what are the things themselves, they cannot tell. The materialist insists on facts, on history, on the force of circumstances, and the animal wants of man; the idealist on the power of Thought and of Will, on inspiration, on miracle, and on individual culture.

These two modes of thinking are both natural, but the idealist contends that his way of thinking is in higher nature. He concedes all that the other affirms, admits the impressions of sense, admits their coherency, their use and beauty, and then asks the materialist for his grounds of assurance that things are as his senses represent them.

The materialist, secure in the certainty of sensation, mocks at fine-spun theories, at star-gazers and dreamers, and believes that his life is solid, that he at least takes nothing for granted, but knows where he stands, and what he does. Yet how easy it is to show him that he is also a phantom walking and working amid phantoms, and that he need only ask a question or two beyond his daily questions, to find his solid universe growing dim and impalpable before his sense. The sturdy capitalist, no matter how deep and square on blocks of Quincy granite he lays the foundations of his banking-house or Exchange, must set it, at last, not on a cube corresponding to the angles of his structure, but on a mass of unknown materials and solidity, red-hot or white-hot perhaps at the core, which rounds off to an almost perfect sphericity, and lies floating in soft air, and goes spinning away, dragging bank and banker with it at a rate of thousands of miles an hour, he knows not whither—a bit of bullet, now glimmering, now darkling through a small cubic space on the edge of an unimaginable pit of emptiness. And this wild balloon, in which his whole venture is embarked, is just a symbol of his whole state and faculty.

[THE IDEALIST] AFFIRMS FACTS not affected by the illusions of sense, facts which are of the same nature as the faculty which reports them, and not liable to doubt; facts which in their first appearance to us assume a native superiority to material facts, degrading these into a language by which the first are to be spoken; facts which it only needs a retirement from the senses to discern.

The idealist, in speaking of events, sees them as spirits. He does not deny the sensuous fact: by no means; but he will not see that alone. He does not deny the presence of this table, this chair, and the walls of this room, but he looks at these things as the reverse side of the tapestry, as the other end, each being a sequel or completion of a spiritual fact which concerns him.

IN THE ORDER OF THOUGHT, the materialist takes his departure from the external world, and esteems a man as one product of that. The idealist takes his departure from his consciousness, and reckons the world an appearance. The materialist respects sensible masses, Society, Government, social art, and luxury, every establishment, every mass, whether majority of numbers, or extent of space, or amount of objects, every social action.

The idealist has another measure, which is metaphysical, namely, the *rank* which things themselves take in his consciousness; not at all the size or appearance. Mind is the only reality, of which men and all other natures are better or worse reflectors. Nature, literature, history, are only subjective phenomena. Although in his action overpowered by the laws of action, and so, warmly cooperating with men, even preferring them to himself, yet when he speaks scientifically, or after the order of thought, he is constrained to degrade persons into representatives of truths. He does not respect labor, or the products of labor, namely property, otherwise than as a manifold symbol, illustrating with wonderful fidelity of details the laws of being; he does not respect government, except as far as it reiterates the law of his mind; nor the church; nor charities; nor arts, for themselves; but hears, as at a vast distance, what they say, as if his consciousness would speak to him through a pantomimic scene.

His thought—that is the Universe. His experience inclines him to behold the procession of facts you call the world, as flowing perpetually outward from an invisible, unsounded center in himself, center alike of him and of them, and necessitating him to regard all things as having a subjective or relative existence, relative to that aforesaid Unknown Center of him.

From this transfer of the world into consciousness, this beholding of all things in the mind, follow easily his whole ethics. It is simpler to be self-dependent. The height, the deity of man, is to be self-sustained, to need no gift, no foreign force. Society is good when it does not violate me; but best when it is likest to solitude. Everything real is self-existent. Everything divine shares the self-existence of Deity.

IT IS A SIGN of our times, conspicuous to the coarsest observer, that many intelligent and religious persons withdraw themselves from the common labors and competitions of the market and the caucus, and betake themselves to a certain solitary and critical way of living, from which no solid fruit has yet appeared to justify their separation. They hold themselves aloof: they feel the disproportion between their faculties and the work offered them, and they prefer to ramble in the country and perish of ennui, to the degradation of such charities and such ambitions as the city can propose to them. They are striking work, and crying out for something worthy to do.

They are lonely; the spirit of their writing and conversation is lonely; they repel influences; they shun general society; they incline to shut themselves in their chamber in the house, to live in the country rather than in the town, and to find their tasks and amusements in solitude. Society, to be sure, does not like this very well; it saith, Whoso goes to walk alone, accuses the whole world; he declareth all to be unfit to be his companions; it is very uncivil, nay, insulting; Society will retaliate.

Meantime, this retirement does not proceed from any whim on the part of these separators; but if anyone will take pains to talk with them, he will find that this part is chosen both from temperament and from principle; with some willingness, too, and as a choice of the less of two evils; for these persons are not by nature melancholy, sour, and unsocial—they are not stockish or brute—but joyous; susceptible, affectionate; they have even more than others a great wish to be loved. Like the young Mozart, they are rather ready to cry ten times a day, "But are you sure you love me?" Nay, if they tell you their whole thought, they will own that love seems to them the last and highest gift of nature; that there are persons whom in their hearts they daily thank for existing—persons whose faces are perhaps unknown to them, but whose fame and spirit have penetrated their solitude—and for whose sake they wish to exist.

To behold the beauty of another character, which inspires a new interest in our own; to behold the beauty lodged in a human being, with such vivacity of apprehension that I am instantly forced home to inquire if I am not deformity itself: to behold in another the expression of a love so high that it assures itself—assures itself also to me against every possible casualty except my unworthiness—these are degrees on the scale of human happiness to which they have ascended; and it is a fidelity to this sentiment which has made common association distasteful to them. They wish a just and even fellowship, or none.

With this passion for what is great and extraordinary, it cannot be wondered at that they are repelled by vulgarity and frivolity in people. They say to themselves, It is better to be alone than in bad company. And it is really a wish to be met—the wish to find society for their hope and religion—which prompts them to shun what is called society. They feel that they are never so fit for friendship as when they have quitted mankind and taken themselves as friend. A picture, a book, a favorite spot in the hills or the woods, which they can people with the fair and worthy creation of the fancy, can give them often forms so vivid that these for the time shall seem real, and society the illusion.

But, to come a little closer to the secret of these persons, we must say that to them it seems a very easy matter to answer the objections of the man of the world, but not so easy to dispose of the doubts and objections that occur to themselves. They are exercised in their own spirit with queries, which acquaint them with all adversity, and with the trials of the bravest heroes.

When I asked them concerning their private experience, they answered somewhat in this wise: It is not to be denied that there must be some wide difference between my faith and other faith; and mine is a certain brief experience, which surprised me on the highway or in the market, in some place, at some time—whether in the body or out of the body, God knoweth—and made me aware that I had played the fool with fools all this time, but that law existed for me and for all; that to me belonged trust, a child's trust and obedience, and the worship of ideas, and I should never be fool more. Well, in the space of an hour, probably, I was let down from this height; I was at my old tricks, the selfish member of a selfish society. My life is superficial, takes no root in the deep world; I ask, When shall I die, and be relieved of the responsibility of seeing a Universe which I do not use? I wish to exchange this flash-of-lightning faith for continuous daylight, this fever-glow for a benign climate.

These two states of thought diverge every moment, and stand in wild contrast. To him who looks at his life from these moments of illumination, it will seem that he skulks and plays a mean, shiftless, and subaltern part in the world. That is to be done which he has not skill to do, or to be said which others can say better, and he lies by, or occupies his hands with some plaything, until his hour comes again.

Much of our reading, much of our labor, seems mere waiting: it was not what we were born for. Any other could do it as well, or better. So little skill enters into these works, so little do they mix with the divine life, that it really signifies little what we do, whether we turn a grindstone, or ride, or run, or make fortunes, or govern the state.

The worst feature of this double consciousness is that the two lives, of the understanding and of the soul, which we lead, really show very little relation to each other, never meet and measure each other: one prevails now, all buzz and din; and the other prevails then, all infinitude and paradise; and, with the progress of life, the two discover no greater disposition to reconcile themselves.

Yet, what is my faith? What am I? What but a thought of serenity and independence, an abode in the deep blue sky? Presently the clouds shut down again; yet we retain the belief that this petty web we weave will at last be overshot and reticulated with veins of the blue, and that the moments will characterize the days.

Patience, then, is for us, is it not? Patience, and still patience. When we pass, as presently we shall, into some new infinitude, out of this Iceland of negations, it will please us to reflect that, though we had few virtues or consolations, we bore with our indigence, nor once strove to repair it with hypocrisy or false heat of any kind.